# IPPOLITA
# IN THE FACEBOOK AQUARIUM
# THE RESISTIBLE RISE OF ANARCHO-CAPITALISM

*Revised and updated edition*

Theory on Demand #15
**The Facebook Aquarium: The Resistible Rise of Anarcho-Capitalism**


Author: Ippolita
Translated by: Patrice Riemens and Cecile Landman
Copy-editing: Matt Beros
Editorial support: Miriam Rasch
Design: Katja van Stiphout
EPUB development: Gottfried Haider
Printer: Print on Demand
Publisher: Institute of Network Cultures, Amsterdam, 2015
ISBN: 978-94-92302-00-7

*Revised and updated English edition, June 2015.*
First published in Italian as *Nell'acquario di Facebook,* Ledizioni, 2012. Published
in French as *J'aime pas Facebook,* trans. Isabelle Felici, Payot, 2012. English version
originally published as a feuilleton on Nettime, 2014. Supported by the Antenna
Foundation, Nijmegen (http://www.antenna.nl) and Casa Nostra, Vogogna-Ossola, Italy.

**Contact**
Institute of Network Cultures
Phone: +31 20 5951865
Email: info@networkcultures.org
Web: http://www.networkcultures.org

This publication is available through various print on demand services.
For more information, and a freely downloadable PDF: http://networkcultures.org/publications

'I started building an aquarium. It became larger and larger, until I managed to build a saltwater aquarium. Then I stopped and thought, either I walk out, or I go into the aquarium myself.'
— Malcolm

'Hit a straight lick with a crooked stick.'
— Jamaican proverb

# CONTENTS

# IN THE FACEBOOK AQUARIUM
## PRE-AFTERWORD

This essay is a critical investigation of the phenomenon of social media and the so-called Web 2.0. We use the example of Facebook, but most of our analysis is applicable to all the free services on the internet. We want to stress that our approach is anti-prohibitionist. This is not a simple stand 'against' all commercial internet experiences, but a description from a hybrid political and situated approach.

The problem is not the existence of machines in general, and not even digital cameras or social-networks in particular, but specifically these machines that are made to control us, with algorithms designed to record our online activites while generating profit. We have to practice harm reduction and prevention, but we also must use creative skills to introduce heterogeneity, and move like nomads between the folds and crevices. Every tactic is welcome, there are no overall answers or global solutions, but only individual, local paths that can become collective, translated, betrayed and adapted to different realities.

For example, the relationship with the social can be framed in many ways that are useful: with the application of the rules of social media marketing to political communication, with hacking, through desertion, and the construction of the social 'other'. We like the idea of replacing the concept of the social network with the trusted network. We do not need to socialize more, but we need to build organized networks with the people and the machines that we trust.

The difficulty lies in the organization, because as its name implies, it is a kind of 'organic' matter, typical of organisms, and this process of de-corporealization, the delegation of vital-to-the-machines issues, already started long ago. Formation is required for all, since the digital natives are often analog illiterates and almost always digitally naïve users of the internet who don't absorb consumerism antibodies at birth. For a start, they need to be trained to not leave traces on the web, to learn social engineering techniques in order to recognize these when they are applied to them, and to understand their own digital alter egos. They need not be scared of the dangers, nor excited of the compelling professional opportunities offered by the sharing economy; or of even learning how to use commercial devices, or worse still, filling in forms which are destined to enter into the oblivion guaranteed by the Google bureaucracy.

We are available; above all this is an invitation to write to us. It's a perfect time for radical critique. The group Ippolita has long since scattered throughout the world. We come from different disciplines, but we all grew up in the shadow of hacklab and experiences of self-management. We use the cartographic method to describe the morphology of the objects that we examine, depending on each one's point of view.

The legacy of the 20th century has accustomed us to think that social control pertains only to the political, but it has long since become primarily an economic question of commercial implications. It is no coincidence that the NSA has made use of the collaboration with Microsoft, Yahoo, Google, Facebook, Apple and so on, to obtain data for the surveillance program PRISM. Although several companies have claimed to be unaware of the program and have refused to make such information automatically available on a large scale, it is easy to understand how their data storage capacity makes them the only credible partners to expand the scope of espionage. If only for the fact that these companies have been developing specific skills in this field for many years.

The mainstream media have cried foul; indignation about the interference of intelligence agencies, and the US government in particular has spread. It was a historical break, there will be a 'before' and 'after' Datagate. But few really care about where this vast quantity of personal data is stored, this data that every day is filtered through commercial platforms. It is certainly legitimate and necessary to protest the state bureaucracy and detest it, but those who feed the phobia of state, weighing in on the Snowden case and similar ones, may not be aware of the power that lies behind the States, their accomplices, and without them the pervasiveness of PRISM would not have the same effect. We are talking of the digital masters: Google, Amazon, Facebook, Apple and Microsoft are able to conserve our lives as we live them, moment by moment, orchestrating grandiose experiments of social technology where the rules are decided in the laboratory. For example, the alteration of the Facebook newsfeed in the 2014 experiment of emotional contagion which has involved approximately 689,000 unaware users. The Megamachine cannot exist without them.

The platforms are transforming into systems that govern citizens. The overlap of the public plan with social and personal interests is generating extraordinary forms of emotional fusionality. Commercial social networks that are becoming inhabited are being experienced as a collective digital body, a common good that's capable of embodying the global public opinion.

Users who for the first time are putting up with the experience of taking the public at their word do not realize that the places where democracy is being exercised cannot be the same as those where cooking recipes and photos with your hair looking lustrous are being exchanged. Above all, these spaces should not be offered to the public for free by private companies, in exchange for profit. There is a need for separate and dedicated places, where the rules are created by the users themselves. Use rather than attendance is crucial, because democracy is not a form of intellectual tourism, but a concrete practice.

If we want it to be really popular it has to be experienced from the bottom up, in small local groups, so that everyone has time to learn and criticize. The digital *paideia* business is a metaphysical narrative; it all happens in the space of clicks tweets, and posts, the important thing is to participate in this sort of super-consciousness. [1] The plurality of individual thoughts combined and reinforced in a single thought functions as 'the opinion of the Network', which generates a sense of self-acquittal and gratitude.

Historically only the great monotheistic religions have managed such a mass psychical sharing. While the big players are busy flooding global space, new liberal transformations are being overlooked. As you will see in the text that you have before you, it is a variety of reactionary counter-powers, while they are declaring themselves 'libertarian' heroes, they have nothing to do with socialist ideas of freedom, nor with the practices historically recognized as socialist.

---

1    Paideia (παιδεία), refers to the training of the mental and physical faculties in order to produce a
     broad and enlightened outlook. Paideia includes physical, moral and intellectual exercises as well as
     socialization in order for the individual to become a successful member of the polis.

At this point it is important to remember the great success that open source continues to experience. It looked like a technical issue, of how to develop and license but instead it is a political style. The Open Source Initiative was founded in 1998 to promote the spread of non-proprietary software, but has in fact served to channel the radical attitude of the movement of free software with much success. The open attitude, which is open to trade, had the merit of showing the commercial advantage gained by the release of code under liberal licenses like the Creative Commons, which has favored the voluntary free work of millions of users.

To make the source code a public application means making it accessible, not free. At least in theory, because when you find yourself with millions of lines of code, to really be able deal with it, in a hands-on way requires great human and financial resources. Free software instead is free because rather than constraining the applications to a license and preventing its re-appropriation, it refers to a philosophy of freedom.

Freedom is understood as a duty, a commitment and horizon, not an access or opening and much less as an automatic result guaranteed by the proper license. It is a process, not a given. Of course then we have to fall into the practice of this philosophical approach, and unfortunately, it's often a small step from radicalism to fundamentalism. But we know that it is easy to tell them apart.

Authentic radicalism is hindered by an unwavering skepticism about any dogma; with disenchanted irony it observes every call for purity, or nostalgia about a golden age that has never existed. It is willingly silent when confronted with the media noise of the large events; it welcomes the small well curated things. The movement that we call, for convenience's sake, Open Data (which under the same definition collects a number of very different practices) has its technical and cultural origins in something very specific: Open Source. Whether it's fighting against the excessive power of patents, registered trademarks and all forms of the privatization of knowledge, or making the data available that is held by public authorities, we do not tire to point out, again and again, the abyss that exists between Open and Free. Open data does not question the possibility of making profit by making data public. It is a reassurance addressed to the commercial traders: quiet, it's public data, but open, come closer!

Sharing knowledge is undoubtedly a noble cause, but it is sad to note how the banner of freedom of expression and circulation of knowledge does not find a welcome reception, except when it is technologically proven that it can produce profits. Therefore it is very difficult to think that the big companies of the Web 2.0 would accept not taking advantage by experimenting with user data, when even for human knowledge to be available to the public it must follow the laws of the capitalist market. It is therefore obvious that companies like Google are absolutely in favor of open data, content and access.

But even in this case it is not about condemning open source and all its derivative models, since they are without doubt better than a completely closed approach. However, we stress that the debate about technology is in fact dominated by a fixed and seemingly immutable horizon, that of capitalism. Beyond the blackmail of survival, which certainly neither the developers nor the leaders address, is there something we do not want and do not have to sell? What is a common good if it is not something that you do not sell and do not buy? The data managed or held by the governments is similar to the natural heritage of a historic geographical area; in on other words it is as if Italy would put one of its art cities on sale, arguing that it is a necessary and inevitable market opening. The data in question involves the physical bodies, cultural identity, social relations, history and linguistic behavior of real communities.

From this perspective, the push towards an open society, in Popper's sense of the term, highlights the attempt of an emergent high-tech ruling class, capable of leading the current bureaucracy into a new era of radical transparency, in which human data and administrative data will be managed for free by those elites who are able to fully profit from them. But for now the only existing transparency is that of the users, who become more and more machine readable. Transparency applies to the masses, not to the systems of power, governments included. Social engineering underlying the platforms remains concealed or denied, subject to the prophecies of Big Data.

In the language of computers: we need to re-engineer organizational processes and the production of sense. In the world of social business we are all treated like criminals, even if we do not notice. That is to say, we are all subject to the techniques of profiling, the informatics derived from criminal anthropology. Identifying the network of relationships, cataloguing behaviors, understand the desires and fears of users and integrating them into a feedback system (users voluntary improve their own cataloguing) is the mother lode of the so-called Web 2.0. This is an order to create targeted advertising among other things. Personal data is used to make statistical predictions about any request coming from a wealthy client, for commercial or political means. Every time we use a free service we accept its terms of use, which often means fully and unquestionably accepting the ability for external parties to experiment on our digital body and those of other people with whom we are in contact.

We do not care about this digital body, until an account is violated or disabled (or when the analog body dies), and something does not work anymore. Then we realize that there is no one to ask for help; the only option is to turn to those who know a little about these machines, the geeky friend, or worse still, the informatics consultant on duty whom we are beginning to rely on. So we slowly drink the bitter cup of total technological delegation in which we are stuck and we can confirm this every day. Most of us no longer own our data, at least not in name, it is stored somewhere else on cloud services rather than on the hardware that we have at hand. In the Panopticon of the commercial society we compete to generate as much 'authentic' material as possible, in redundant Facebook posts or distilled into smaller and smaller spaces like a perfect 140-character tweet.

Each of us is a unique and changing being and it is this ineffable uniqueness, combined with the desire to emerge, which feeds the machines. The combination of our differences becomes fuel for bio-political control, and we simply become biomass. In this way capitalism can extract value directly from the human capacity to generate meaning, regardless of the distinctions between sex, race, age and social belonging. By subjecting a diverse range of individuals to profiling algorithms it becomes possible to improve the system of prediction, indefinitely. In all this there is nothing new that the legacy of the 20th century had not already delivered, at least in theoretical form. No apocalypse, we are still very much in the old Europe and despite everything we have the necessary tools to recognize and challenge the formation of toxic narratives like this. The prophecies of the self-realization of Big Data were already around in Delphi five hundred years before Christ, when predictions in the form of prophecy had become a political device.

Unable to stop the moving train just a few will decide to get off. An economic-social class division is beginning to take shape at the horizon, not only in regard to the constant and sterile threats to net neutrality, an absurd logic that never existed and can not exist, just like privacy, but also in the sense of access to services. On the one hand there will be those of the A type, partially protected and paid for by the elite who understood that using Gmail to manage their own affairs is a bad idea; on the other hand those of the B-type, the uneducated masses, shaped by social media filled with advertising and subjected to marketing and profiling. The dynamics of privacy by payment could be the same as the old virus and anti-virus model: who produces the former will also produce the latter.

We are not alone, there are those who begin to smell a rat, and have already been working for some time on digital self-defense. Self-defense is to be self-consciousness, of one's own history and proper limits, a way of learning how to manage personal resources in a common world. To transform personal vulnerabilities into many strengths, without yielding to a militaristic, Manichean narrative. For example, many teachers, educators and trainers have found that to intervene in the study of technology in order to train individuals, it is necessary to recognize that commercial platforms should be structured as pedagogical settings. They are beginning to criticize the system in ontological terms.

Technologies are tools, not data. All technologies embody and incorporate the ideologies of the people who created them. In the case of highly complex and popular technologies, the ideological effects appear as always in place, i.e. natural conditions, while in fact they are absolutely artificial consequences of the adoption of those tools. We met those involved to convey the passion for knowledge, halfway between philosophy and technique, creating workshops and playing, to imagine a new digital *paideia*. We found that a motivated teacher can be as determined as a hacker.

As we said at the beginning, this is above all an invitation to write, discuss, and make direct action. It's a perfect time for radical critique.


Ippolita, Naples, 2015
Translated by Cecile Landman

# PART I:
# I HAVE A THOUSAND FRIENDS, BUT I KNOW NO ONE

## 1.01 — DEFAULT POWER, OR PLEASE FOLLOW THE INSTRUCTIONS

Facebook has now almost reached the one billion users mark worldwide, Windows Live Messenger, Twitter and LinkedIn host 350 million, 330 million and 130 million accounts, respectively. [1] Google+ has also made a splash in the market. These numbers are constantly rising, while new social networks appear almost daily. This phenomena is not exclusive to Western or democratic societies; tens of millions of Russians have an account with Vkontakte; Chinese social networks like Qzone and Renren, which are closely controlled by the authorities, have over one hundred million users; the Iranian government sponsors Cloob, etc. An overwhelming majority of all these users accept the default settings of the platforms offered by the social networks. When these settings are modified, as often happens (e.g. in 2010 when Facebook revised its privacy settings, not once, but several times) almost all users adopt the new settings without dissent. This is what we call 'default power': the ability to change the online lives of millions of users by simply tweaking a few parameters. For the networks owners anything is possible, whether it is closing down the pages of cat lovers or censoring risqué photos.

Next time we log on our online profile may appear radically different, as if the décor in our home had suddenly been rearranged. We should always remember that when we talk about 'mass social media', nobody wants to be part of this mass. But when we use these networks we are the 'mass' and the mass is subject to default power.

## 1.02 — IN THE BEGINNING WAS GOOGLE

In early 2006, when the Social Web was just for the select few (in the US, Ivy League universities and Stanford were just beginning to embrace Facebook), Ippolita published *Open non è free* ('Open Does not Mean Free'). [2] We argued open source and free software are not the same thing. Freedom comes at a cost while opening up to the market can be highly profitable. Our reception was modest at best, as our approach was largely philosophical at the expense of simplicity. This is because it was becoming apparent that we were witnessing a paradigm shift in the digital world from epistemology to ontology. The 'what' (what you know) was rapidly replaced by the 'who' (what you are). In other words, management of knowledge was becoming management (and construction) of identity.

But the subject matter was of paralyzing complexity, and worse still, of little interest to the general public. Debating the transformations in IT for the benefit of a handful of specialists was a pointless exercise. Therefore our new task became a critique of the largest actor in its domain,

---

1    All statistics in this translation are reproduced from the original Italian edition: Ippolita, *Nell'acquario di Facebook,* Milan: Ledizioni, 2012.

2    Ippolita, *Open non è free,* Milan: Eleuthera, 2005.

the most popular and versatile search engine, Google. Google's mission, a dogma preached by many digital evangelists, is the organization of all of the information in the world. As stated by Eric Schmidt, the former CEO of the Mount View giant, Google is a global IT enterprise valued at 'a hundred billion US dollars'.

But Google is just one example of what is becoming increasingly common, namely people delegating their '(re)search choices' to a hegemonic subject. Google's vision of the future finds its clearest expression in the 'I am feeling lucky' button: a technocratic subject who shares my desires and realizes them. I am what Google knows of me: I trust Google with everything; my ontology is Google's epistemology. My online searches and browsing, my contacts and my preferences, my emails, pictures, private and public messages; everything that makes up my identity is being taken care of, managed 'for my own good', by Google.

Thanks to its copyleft distribution, *The Dark Side of Google*, has been translated in several languages. [3] Yet, even as Google is still very much discussed, no new analysis has managed to overcome specialist concerns and address the larger public. On the other hand, there are an increasing number of studies published on indexing algorithms and manuals on Google's ten new services that enable users to generate wealth. But nobody has attempted to break through the banality of the new service documentation. Cloud computing is now affected by FOG (Fear of Google), the dread that an information monopoly becomes a threat, not only to individuals, but also to private companies, state institutions and international bodies. But what is actually being feared? There is a growing angst about the possibility of an emerging rhizomatic control by businesses and administrations, (in earlier times we would have said the military-industrial complex). Semi-authoritarian governments, but also anti-trust commissions, firms and individuals have taken Google to court in cases where millions of dollars are at stake. Yet, in the age of the triumphant 'free market', it shouldn't be that difficult to grasp the fact that 'gratuity' means that the services provided have to be funded from somewhere else: in this case through increasingly perfected control. Someone must be able to 'know it all', in order for sophisticated account holders to 'own' their unique, customized object, and feel really 'free'.

Has anything changed since 2006? Not really, the dozen or so new services offered by Google have only confirmed the totalitarian nature of a project aimed at 'organizing all the world's information'. Google embodies more than ever the global 'webization' of the Net. Its weapons are always the same, simplicity and efficiency, academic-inspired 'excellence' (Stanford, Silicon Valley), soft capitalism (rewards, brand and corporate identity), exploitation of open source code, etc. Sure, Google now seems old, panting to keep up with the 'new actors of the Web 2.0' and belatedly joining the 'social networking' fray. The 'good giant' definitely did take a 'social' turn with Google+ but only after the catastrophic failure of Google Wave and Google Buzz. Google+ 'circles' (of relationship) were promptly copied by Facebook in an attempt to silence its critics regarding the rather tricky subject of its privacy management. In the meanwhile, more aggressive competitors have gained positions of power.

---

3    Ippolita, *The Dark Side of Google*, trans. Patrice Riemens, Amsterdam: Institute of Network Cultures, Theory on Demand #13, 2013. Available from: http://networkcultures.org/blog/publication/no-13-the-dark-side-of-google-ippolita/.

## 1.03 — THE ERA OF DEMOCRATIC DISTRACTION-ATTENTION

Web 2.0 refers more to a new mode of behavior than a set of new technologies. We must stay online all the time in order to: chat with friends, post pictures, text, videos etc., share everything with your *community*, stay connected, be part of the 'zeitgeist' of the online world. [4] 'In a word we must 'share'. Perhaps the greatest hoax ever invented and yet, one that has had extraordinary success. Emails, IRC chats, blogs, mailing lists, feeds, peer-to-peer, VoIP... Wasn't that enough to share? No, because according to the belief in unlimited growth, which is the gospel of Californian turbo-capitalism, one always needs more, bigger (or smaller but more powerful), faster. We are all afflicted yet enthusiastic followers of today's ideology. Our new phone is more powerful than our old desktop computer and our laptop has a greater capacity than the old server at work. Our new email allows us to send attachments larger than all our previous messages combined and our new camera has better resolution than our old TV.

With Facebook, the ideology of 'we want it all but faster!' has entered a new, quasi-religious phase. Salvation is the promise and 'share and thou shalt be happy' is the message. With over nine hundred millions users in May 2012 (i.e. the population of Europe and the US combined) exponential growth, a global phenomena yet organized in groups of 'friends', Facebook could not escape the attention of Ippolita. A radical critique of Facebook is essential, not only because we should always aim for the largest target but also because it informs the tactical approach of Ippolita. We want to develop new technological instruments of self-management and autonomy, not imposed by the dictates of a refined theory, but with a basis in daily use, abuse and subversion of the technologies that built our current networked world.

Now, if you are Facebook addict (or LinkedIn, MySpace, Groupon, Twitter, etc.) to the point of not being willing to take a closer look at what is happening behind the scenes, then perhaps you should stop reading here. Our aim is not to convince you that Facebook is evil, but to use it as an example to understand the present. This is not an objective investigation, on the contrary it is subjective, partisan and based on a very clear assumption: Web 2.0 lead by Facebook, is a phenomena of technocratic delegation and is therefore dangerous. It doesn't matter whether the instruments themselves are good or bad, or whether we love or hate them, and it doesn't matter whether we are captive and deluded users or tech savvy geeks.

The key assumption that underlies all research conducted by Ippolita is very simple: to connect to a network means tracing a line between a point of origin and another point. In a sense, it is the same as opening up one's window to another world. It is not always easy to engage in exchanges or to open up, because neither is immediate or natural. Specific skills need to be developed to suit your personal needs and capacities. There is also no such thing as absolute security – the only real security is to avoid connecting at all. But since we want to get in touch with others and because we want to create tools to make this possible, we are not renouncing connectivity. On the other hand, we will not passively adopt all 'new' technology as a tool for liberation.

The 'rhizomatic' diffusion of social networks creates its own dynamic of inclusion and exclusion, the same as we witnessed during the boom of mobile phones. People without a Facebook account

---

4    Ippolita, Geert Lovink and Ned Rossiter, 'The Digital Given. 10 Theses on Web 2.0', *The Fiberculture Journal 14* (2009), http://fourteen.fibreculturejournal.org/fcj-096-the-digital-given-10-web-2-0-theses/.

are part of no community at all, or more radically: they simply do not exist, and it becomes difficult for them to keep in touch. This is especially true for those who haven't started building relationships before the magical era of social networks. Teenagers, therefore, face even more peer pressure to adopt these new technologies exclusively, at the expense of other modes of communication. On the bright side, they are usually more savvy and competent at handling these technologies than adults. Being born into a digitally networked world, they know the advantages and drawbacks through firsthand experience. On the downside, they usually lack historical memory, mistakenly believing that they are completely different from the generations that preceded them and therefore face problems that require totally new tools to solve them. But being ridiculed on your Facebook wall is not so different from the teasing that occurs among all teenagers regardless of the period or culture. Social issues are human issues before anything else: they are always specific to relationships and the public environment. Despite high resolution and touch-screens, 'civilization 2.0' looks very much like all civilizations, which preceded it, as human beings have always felt the need to attract each other's attention. Humans still need to eat, sleep, maintain friendships, and give meaning to the world they inhabit. They still fall in love, experience disappointments, hope, dream, err, harm or kill each other. In other words, humans deal with the consciousness that their existence has its limits both in time (the horrible reality of death) and in space (the scandal that there are *others* and a world outside) – even in the era of digital social networks. We will see that in the time of global distraction-attention it has become more difficult to develop and implement suitable policies, as everyone is constantly busy chatting, publishing, tweeting, instagramming etc., so much so, that there is no time left to cultivate meaningful relationships.

Despite the fact that body and language define the limits of human experience, an important part of the adult population still refuses to learn how to use digital technologies in a responsible way. Frightened by the prospect of not being able to keep up in a society that has fallen victim to a rampant 'cult of the youth' while continuing to be ruled by gerontocrats with facelifts, many adults simply don't want to get their hands dirty with digital technologies. People who are active socially (in 'real life'): often hide behind a kind of demotivated 'I don't understand a thing' -attitude, which comes close to a new form of Luddism. This perception of having to work with something totally new is further aggravated by the uncanny enthusiasm of technophiles, who are advocates of internet-centrism, a belief that everybody and everything is destined to pass through the Web, whether it's about interpersonal relationships, buying and selling, local and international politics, health, or education. For the technophile, Web 2.0 is the realization of a perfect world, where every *netizen* contributes to the common good, primarily as a consumer.

Cyber-utopians come in many denominations. The most rabid conservatives are the cold war nostalgics, who are still convinced that the Soviet block collapsed during the autumn of 1989 as if by magic, thanks to the pressure exercised by CIA-sponsored free radio stations, and as result of the dissemination of clandestine pro-Western publications enabled by the new technologies of the day (photocopiers and fax machines). In other words, those regimes were defeated by the freedom of information. Apparently an explanation of events where the West's freedom of information triumphed over Soviet tyranny is preferable to considering the economic and political dead ends inherent to that system, the mistakes made by it's rulers or combing through the pre-glasnost archives. The approved narrative is that people behind the Iron Curtain suddenly discover that the emperor has no clothes, the pro-regime guns would never be aimed at them, and most importantly Western supermarkets were laden with such wonders as to embolden anyone who had to put up with the shoddy wares of the communist dictatorships. So the people submissive to the diktats of the Warsaw pact became enlightened by the subversive Western media and rebelled to gain access to the free market.

Having established capitalism as the one and only way, the conservatives seemingly found themselves with no more enemies to fight. The end of history, as preached by ultra-liberal like Francis Fukuyama, was only a sad realization in the alluring landscape of 1990s global consumerism. But China did not collapse after the Tiananmen Square events on the contrary it launched a dynamic race into capitalism, while keeping its despotic regime in place. Real-time Western media did not bring democracy but did enable Westerners to feel part of the global spectacle while remaining ensconced in their living room couches. The Gulf War was instantly broadcasted courtesy of CNN and later the 'Arab Spring' could be (re)lived thanks to Facebook and Twitter. With a few exceptions, the old dictators are still in power while a few new ones have made their appearance on all continents. This is all good news for cyber-warmongers, because digital warfare looks ever more essential to the triumph of the 'free market'.

Conservative cyber-utopians are easy to spot. They will tell you that the Web 2.0 communication tools are the freedom missiles aimed at the heart of totalitarian regimes. They eulogize Iranian, Egyptian, Tunisian, Syrian, and Cuban bloggers (among others) portraying these as pro-Western agents and guerilla-fighters for the free market, endangering them far more than they would be otherwise. They financially sponsor foundations and info-war programs, to defeat modern dictatorship through the power of free of expression, spread counter-repressive systems which disrupt censorship and provoke the uprising of the oppressed masses.

Progressive cyber-utopians are less at ease with military metaphors, yet they still talk about internet freedom as a key concept that needs to be underwritten by governments pretending to aim for a more free and just society. Convinced that the free flow of information is a major instrument for democracy, they are Web 2.0's democratic evangelists. Insofar as users themselves generate most of the content, they contend that democracy will follow all by itself, as a kind of collateral benefit of the internet. In their view the rhizomatic spread of digital automation in society shall automatically lead to global democracy.

Whether they are progressives or conservatives the 'internet gurus' are spreading the perverse logic of social cybernetics where participation in Web 2.0 inevitably generates the conditions for a more developed level of democracy. As with all progressivist beliefs, this is based on the assumption of a linear history, benevolent progress, and that this progression can be quantified. In this simple utopian vision, online participation is to democracy as the GDP is to the well being of society. The era of freedom has arrived and authoritarian regimes are collapsing by the power of a few pointed tweets. Meanwhile, Western societies are becoming more democratic by the day, as citizens are ever better informed, and can access the 'truth' 24/7, thanks to digital networks privately managed for the common good. Connected citizens are totally protected against the abusive behavior of corrupt governments, the manipulation by marketing firms, the propaganda unleashed by religious, nationalist or xenophobic extremists, the hidden violence of certain types of social relations (e.g. *stalking*), and finally, blackmail and organized crime. The cybercitizen always chooses responsibly. Ignorance is a residual problem and wars are simply caused by a lack of information. Even hunger and poverty will be 'solved' thanks to information abundance and free connections that are made possible in this great space of freedom that is the internet.

Today, we are immersed in the knowledge society. We are told that networks make it possible for information to flow freely, as is the case for money, and we are being promised that these flows of information will bring us wellbeing, wealth, and happiness. We have moved from the wealth of nations to the wealth of networks: democracy at the global scale, connection at the local scale. But even a quick look at the reality surrounding us shows us that cyber-utopianism is a delusion never mind the ongoing financial and economic crisis. Democracy 2.0 has nothing to do with an open, liberal society and even less so with a revolutionary society made up of autonomous individuals, capable of managing a world based on non-authoritarian dynamics. On the contrary, Society 2.0 disturbingly resembles the 'closed society' the liberal philosopher Karl Popper was describing as the counterpart to Western democracy.

The enthusiasm around social networks is a classic phenomenon that can be witnessed every time a new media technology makes it appearance. With every new wave of technological innovation, there is an influx of 'experts' and futurists revealing the hidden logic of this or that technology. So first we had the press, which was believed to be the absolute bulwark of democracy in Europe; then as the telegraph system emerged, war came to be seen as an absurdity belonging to an earlier dark age where people could not communicate. Later we were made to believe that radio, a promising technology which at least in theory, should enable everybody not only to receive broadcasts but also to broadcast themselves, would be the crucial tool for a new era of peace. Finally, television held the promise of exhibiting to all what was happening in remote regions of the world: the horrors of war, now to be witnessed in real time, would be averted. Yet religious wars have erupted since, and this is specifically thanks to a press bringing modern nationalists and state bureaucrats all the support they were lacking. The telegraph was one of the major instruments which brought North American Indians to their near-extinction in the 'Far West'. The radio (broadcast) was the most powerful propaganda weapon in the hands of fascists and the Nazi regime. The same phenomena can be observed in the genocides in former Yugoslavia and in Rwanda. The television functions both as an anesthesia of the masses and a pulpit for the most aggressive type of (tele)evangelists.

Media euphoria is never a good thing, because it is based on the idea of technological determinism and a faith in the Enlightenment tradition for which knowledge is emancipatory and revolutionary. This is why we are repeatedly told that information is empowering, that knowledge and ideas are revolutionary per se and that progress is inevitable. So why worry anymore when communication means are *ipso facto* democratic? The long awaited-for revolution has taken place through the social media which enables every individual to personally participate in the construction of society. Technological determinism is based on an assumed 'historical necessity' in which individual choices amount to nothing. In this respect it is akin to Marxist dialectics: freedom will impose itself by necessity, since technology is free in itself, and heralds universal human rights, independently of the people involved – just as the dictatorship of the proletariat is inescapable. This hides the fact that the firms behind the social media boom are not working unconsciously to bring about an unavoidable historical process, but are, on the contrary, actively pursuing their own vested interests. It is not the case that privacy is an outdated idea simply because society is moving towards the total transparency its technology prescribes. Facebook, Google, Twitter, Amazon, etc. are the actors bent on abolishing privacy so they can introduce the reign of customized consumption.

Evgeny Morozov is among those rare authors to have warned against the dirty tricks of the Net, as well as against technology-worship and internet-centrism. The Belarusian author reminds us that the essence of technology is not technological, but can only be analyzed in terms of sociology, economics, political science, psychology or anthropology. It is therefore absurd to think of the internet as an independent, solely technological object, that can absorb any other media discourse.

More an Aristotelian property rather than a Kantian category, technology is a master key of conceptual and discursive discourses, as the technological object appears to embody a virtuous attribute, the technologicity, a manifestation of a technological idea. This ideal finds it natural environment in the hi-tech object. This is an attribute entirely devoid of concrete meaning, just as if horsiness was an attribute unique to horses and humanity unique to human beings. We need to consider these issues without take refuge in obscure statements.

It is often argued that it is all about the use of a technology, since in itself, a technology is neutral. This is a fallacy. Technology is anything but neutral. Every tool has specific characteristics that need to be analyzed. In other words, technology embeds and incorporate the beliefs, the ideas and the ideologies of people who build that technology. That's why they're not neutral, and that's why we can retrace an archeology of technologies analyzing the archives of these technologies in the sense of Foucault's archive and archaeology. But it is also useful to look at the issue in its general context. Technology goes with power, and the usage of technological instruments implies a competence, which is the outcome of specialized knowledge. This puts the user in a dynamic of power: 'in relation to'. Even using a technology is not neutral because it alters the identity of its user, e.g. a plumber derives his identity as a plumber from his power-knowledge of plumbing technology. An essential point to understand is that the communication tools, specifically designed for online socializing, not only alters the identity of the users, but also the identity of the community as a whole. The use of communication technology in a social context is a source of social power, we term 'socio-power'. By this term we mean the following:

> (...) the conditioning forces which shape the relations between individuals and collectivities. These forces express themselves in the 'devices' which are now embedded in everyday socialization i.e. all those moments where subjectivity relates to common sense, behavior norms, judgment criteria, notions of belonging and exclusion, and the concept of deviance. (...) Power activates the mechanisms and certain types of outcomes (i.e. the creation of a particular behavior) which are analogous to those produced by the socialization process. The differences depend on the 'devices' being used. While power is usually visualized in specific moments, socio-power is more holistic, invasive, and ubiquitous. Socio-power effects the organization of knowledge and the regulation of practices. Therefore it should not exclusively be seen as the power to alter another person's behavior by force. On the contrary, it is a much more subtle, ability to shape a given course of action and to promote or discourage certain dispositions. [5]

Seen from this perspective, we have distanced ourselves noticeably from Morozov's position who, as befits a good and sincere democrat, really believes that Western governments are on a mission to export democracy all over the world. As socio-power is so invasive it becomes necessary to abandon the analysis of large oppressive systems (governments, big business, international politics) in

---

5    Stefano Boni, *Cuture e Poteri*, Milan: Eleuthera, 2011, pp. 29-33.

order to focus on small fissures and deviances that form lines of flight. So let us not limit ourselves to a mere critique of the interference of social media in today's society, as if it were Facebook's fault that people now only communicate through virtual channels. We need to dig deeper, is it only because the users themselves are welcoming this interference and making it possible? Our analysis should keep a proper perspective on those large, oppressive actors who appear to be dominant and representative of this Zeitgeist of the knowledge society. Let us refrain from thinking that every new technological gadget is potentially a tool of empowerment and democratization. We should remind ourselves that it might also be a formidable tool of oppression as well. Therefore, we will try to shed light, a bit like an archeologist, on the historical, political, and economic rationale behind Facebook's assertion that sharing is the panacea that will cure all society's ills. However we will keep in mind Morozov's acute analyses on the ease with which authoritarian regimes have adopted the philosophy of Web 2.0 in order to better control their population. The fact remains that new modalities of relationship between individuals are emerging and they call for a specific analytical approach. So let us now go into the details of what we do not like about Web 2.0, and Facebook in particular.

## 1.04 — SOCIAL DYNAMICS: VOYEURISM AND HOMOPHILIA

Facebook promotes 'homophily', the mutual fascination experienced by those who feel they share a common identity — which has nothing to do with affinity. [6] Facebook 'Friends' are, at least formally, people who come together because they 'like' the same things: 'this is what we like' is what they express. Perhaps in the future they will add 'this is what we don't like'. But the latter is unlikely, since dissent provokes discussion. So we take part in the same events. We are equals, and that is why we feel happy together and we exchange notes, messages, 'presents', games, and pokes. Social exchange is organized on the basis of the identity. Dialectics is impossible, conflict is banned by design and evolution (intersection, exchange and selection of differences) is obstructed. We stick together because we recognize ourselves to belong to the same identity. Deviance is out, diversity is a non-issue, and actually, we are not concerned in the least.

From a social viewpoint, homophilia leads to the tendency of generating monolithic groups of people who literally all echo each other. It is precisely the opposite of affinity, where difference, on the contrary is a condition. Difference here is even prized as the starting point of every relationship. In affinity-based relationships, individuals perceive each other and engage in relationships as the outcome of a bundle of differences which suggest likeness, facilitating easier interactions. There is no such thing as a requirement to adjust to the group, since it is the uniqueness of the individual that creates value, not his conformity within the group.

The logical outcome of social structuring in small homogenous groups, consisting in a few hundred 'friends' or a few thousands 'fans' is the emergence of social dynamics akin to those of a village. Everybody knows everything about everybody else. Social control is pervasive and implicit in every relationship. Even if it is possible, in theory, to set up different levels of sharing of the information published on our profile, the actual practice is to have everything published without restriction, and as this spreads out further and further afield, 'total transparency' on 'the whole

---

6    Miller McPherson, Lynn Smith-Lovin and James M. Cook, 'Birds of a Feather: Homophily in Social Networks', *Annual Review of Sociology*, vol 27: 415-444, August 2001, http://www.annualreviews.org/doi/abs/10.1146/annurev.soc.27.1.415.

internet' is attained. As per company policy, Facebook is based on the concept of sharing, and is designed to allow you to connect with and find others more easily.[7] The underlying economic rationale of this, which we will elaborate in more detail, is obvious: 'encouraging people to become public increases advertising revenues. [...] Technology makes everything more visible and accessible. The technology is completely aligned with the market.'[8]

The ideology of sharing on Web 2.0 makes exposure of others a fully acceptable and encouraged social practice and self-exposure the golden rule of community life. Rob was yesterday at Alice's party, here are the pics, 'like' them and share them with all your 'friends'. Update your profile and tell everybody what you 'like', where you are with whom, and what you are doing. Please tell us what is your favorite brand of jeans, and what's your favorite position in bed, with full details. You're looking for this great lube with that special taste, now here we've got a customized ad just for you, matching your requirements precisely, and available now!

When a group's identity is established on the basis of feelings so simple as to be captured by the 'Like' button, iterating over and again what one 'likes' becomes essential. But on the other hand it is also crucial to know in real time what other people 'like' so as to avoid unpleasant discrepancies with the common identity that reinforces our sense of belonging. To cement the group identity implies control of others as well as self-control. Articulating a strong dislike of this or that, is out of the question, just as are nasty pronouncements about this or that person who is one of the 'friends' of some of our 'friends'. Just ignoring is the right option. In these types of relationships, creative conflict is replaced with indifference but also a subtle nastiness where people take pleasure in posting the least flattering photos of their 'friends'. This creates an underground relational accounting system, where we react almost instantly to those who are respond quickly, while sharing invitations, comment requests and 'like' with others are simply left as an afterthought.

Facebook offers many tools to track all the activities of users. Facebook Connect and Facebook Mobile make it easy to stay connected even when users are logged on Facebook, or in front of a computer screen. The spread of self-exposure devices like smartphones and tablets enables further cross-collecting of geo-referenced GSM data together with increasingly detailed personal profiles on social networks. All of this is for our own good, in order to let us share more, faster and better. But do we really share?

## 1.05 — PSYCHOLOGICAL DYNAMICS: NARCISSISM, EXHIBITIONISM, AND EMOTIONAL PORN

The first thing we share on Facebook is obviously our own identity, be it through our real name, or, possibly, an avatar. Date of birth and sex, at the moment two options only, male or female – must be provided, to prevent the registration of children under thirteen. In practice, whatever name is given is almost always the true first and surname. As the homepage states as a welcome 'Facebook enables you to connect and share with people in your life'. It is of course easier to trace somebody if she uses her 'real' identity.

---

7    See, https://www.facebook.com/help/search/?query=real%20names.
8    Erica Naone, 'The Changing Nature of Privacy on Facebook', *MIT Technology Review*, May 2010, http://www.technologyreview.com/news/418766/the-changing-nature-of-privacy-on-facebook/.

Facebook doesn't like fake names, since it's network profiles itself as 'a community where people use their real identities'. We require everyone to provide their real names, so you always know who you're connecting with. This helps keep our community safe.' 'The security of our community is very important to us. Hence we will delete any account registered under a false name as soon as we discover them. [9] Ippolita, being a collective that uses an heteronym while promoting the creation of multiple identities can only repudiate such an approach. Moreover, from a biological point of view, an individual's identity is always mutating, and a name and a place of birth are a fairly limited as an identifier of a human being. The self presents itself to the world as a theatre play. Identity is a permanently under construction, it is neither stable nor unchanging. Only the dead are fixed, living beings are not – that's why they are living. [10] But for now we will dispense of the philosophical aspects of identity, and focus on what makes up the negotiation of virtual identity.

The profile picture we choose is highly important. Therefore we should post a photograph that shows us under the most favorable angle and arouses interest in the viewer. This is our 'True Me', not those pictures where we look tired, bored – or drunk. Embarrassing pictures are those of others, which we will seek out, in accordance with the dynamics of exposure and self-exposure. Everyone wants to present their best face while seeking out the defects in others with unhealthy abandon. On Facebook we are all Narcissus looking at his own image as reflected by the social network. Hence it is important to hide what is embarrassing and unfit to be told, as it risks making one un-'liked'. Since Facebook had been originally conceived as a speed-dating site, albeit one geared to 'fish' in the largest possible 'pond' (yet in the very elitist manner of the Ivy League universities, now transformed into a kind of 'mass elitism'), it is clear that in order to achieve the maximum dating score, it is essential to show your very best face. [11]

The second movement in the mirror is the image that reflects itself. We reflect in order to please ourselves, not in order to complain. But Narcissus' mirror image can only be a form of exhibitionism taken to the extreme. Compulsive use is characteristic of the discovery of a new game, especially when the game's rules require total self-disclosure – though the more obscene parts should be censored, since it is well-known that Facebook will terminate accounts if found to host pictures of naked bodies. Celebrity demands some sacrifices, yet even micro-celebrity, the currency of Facebook, can only be obtained through exhibitionism. Fans must always be able to connect with their micro-idol.

In the society of the spectacle, we are all at the same time applauding spectators, and actors on the stage playing the role of our virtual identities. It is impressive how much personal details people are prepared to disclose just to get some attention. It is easy to demonstrate that social network constitute a remarkable arena of self-exhibitionist masturbation. Create a Facebook account with a believable first name and surname (neither too common nor too obviously false)

---

9    See, https://www.facebook.com/help/245058342280723.

10   See François Laplantine, in particular: *Je, Nous et les autres. Etres humains au-delà des appartenances,* Paris: Le Pommier, 1999 and *Le Sujet: essai d'anthropologie politique,* Paris: Éditions Téraèdre, 2007.

11   Mass elitism is an oxymoron which is the basis for many advertising campaigns. The most prized products are sold 'exclusively' for low prices because 'luxury is a right'. See Gruppo MARCUSE, *Miseria Humana Della Publicità,* Milan: Eleuthera, 2006.

open an email address (created on Google, and linked to all mailing lists, newsletters and RSS feeds your alter ego should be interested in), list where you went to college, name the football team you're a fan of, music you like and what your hobbies are. Send as many friendship requests as possible, Facebook will help you discover scores of new 'friends' you'd never known they existed. Answer with enthusiasm to those you want to befriend you, send them links to LOLcats, offer to take care of their farmville – and you will be rewarded with plenty of attention. [12] With a bit of 'engineering' you can discover all you wish to know about your new 'friends'.

For some time now, software programs have been used on social networks, giving users full mastery of the golden rules of social engineering. These programs 'study' people's behavior in order to extract useful information. They behave just as if they know things, make errors, and lie. In this way socialbots have been able to penetrate and compromise networks of trust on Facebook. But there are also less sophisticated approaches that exist. Phishing for instance, is a widespread attack method, based on social engineering. To trap prey, you need only to issue a warning like 'alert! your Facebook account is under attack! Log in here now to change your password!'. This way, even data that have not been shared with everybody become accessible.

The resulting paradox becomes apparent; we live in a world where everyone is forced to be authentic, to tell the truth about what they do and love, to reveal their exact location and at the same time, the opportunity opens for a predatory person to use the same tools to be completely artificial and deceptive. The predatory user is in an ideal situation where they are surrounded by a near infinite pool of overly trusting, attention starved people. Andy Warhol predicted that everybody would get her or his fifteen minutes of fame in the end – but this is far worse than anything imaginable. We are now in the age of diffuse celebrity, accessible to anyone, but with very uncertain limits and demanding a relentless updating of our online profile. We are required to have a total trust in and transparency towards machines which know us better than we know ourselves and advises us on products designed especially for us.

The final stage of psychological involution on Facebook is emotional and relational porn. [13] As talk shows and reality TV aptly demonstrate, hair pulling, crying, shouting, quarreling in public and exchanging insults, in front of a voting public is a source of perverse pleasure. Even a total nobody feels famous. No need for any specific talent in dancing, playing, singing or speaking in public – or to be even be beautiful. A spectacle of unfiltered emotions in front of the camera's gaze is enough. Facebook has intensified this worldwide project of emotional porn by introducing transparency tools in the form of boxes to be clicked on, forms to be completed and empty spaces to be filled with content. What's your current marital status? It's essential that everybody knows whether you are available, engaged, or divorced and ready for adventure. Share your innermost feelings! What are your thoughts right now? Be transparent!

---

12   *Farmville* is one of the most popular games on Facebook, created by the gaming company Zynga, with millions of users. The game simulates the life of a farmer, allowing players to grow plants trees and breed virtual cattle. Objects may be exchanged, gifted, bought and sold.

13   Pornography, from the Greek, ϖ    *porne*, 'prostitute' and        *graphein* 'write' or 'record'. Public representation itself, as a form of narcissistic pleasure, has the traits of self-prostitution. An object in the public market of identity, involves prostitution in exchange for attention.

The most amusing aspect, if it were not so tragic, is the prevalent 'blog style' format, which makes that yesterday's news irrelevant today, allows no clear division of time. Hence, 'experience' is relegated into a kind of ever-lasting present. The past sinks inexorably into an obscure part of cyberspace, and nobody ever reads the older entries, except to seek out the failings. After all, everybody's got something to hide and social relations are based on discretion and lies, or at least, on half-truth and omissions. But an employer, a suspicious partner, a spyware program, or a government to whom Facebook has sold your data would very much like to know more about your previous life. Since you've 'shared' everything with such zeal, they will get all they want in no time. Facebook's introduction of the 'Timeline' feature, where users can insert images, notes, and contents relating to the period before they had an account, answers to the same logic; namely, to make all aspects of someone's personality visible, in a clear, linear and sequential fashion

Here we require no depth, and no complexity, no ambiguity. We can merely be. Non-being simply vanishes, and 'becoming' is simply a category outside the order. Contrary to what happens in the outside world, things within social networks simply are there, they do not 'become'. A new state is superimposed on the previous one, and the previous state is simply deleted – permanently. Your identity is fixed, even if it changes. What do you prefer, males or females? Both? No, that's not allowed, you can tick one box only! Transgender you say? I cannot parse that. Perhaps program-mers are working on new categories for the next version of the software. But if you've changed your mind, no problem. Here's a new identity and a fresh 'status', that annuls all the previous ones. In reality however, identities are complex bundles of qualities which are mutating, sometimes painfully, because the memory of who we were is built upon a process of forgetting, selection, and narrative, and not on the total recall of a fixed profile. [14] Facebook is the champion of emotional and relational porn: be transparent! Write, draw, take photos and make links with what concerns you in the most intimate manner, show your emotions in the most candid way possible, for a public that observes you in the most trivial way possible: this is freedom of expression.

## 1.06 THE PERFORMANCE SOCIETY
Sharing on Facebook essentially means sharing digital 'objects' which make up virtual identities. I am my online behavior. But spending so much time creating an online image of the self has consequences in life off-line. The virtual identities users can construct with Facebook's tools are generally 'flat': they lack the depth of real identities, which are rich in shades and nuances. In real life, before blurting out what we 'really think', you generally weigh up the pros and cons. We don't just storm into the street to shout out that we have been dumped via SMS and are now available again on the meat market. Facebook demands – unfiltered action and this 'sincerity' – often amounts to naive stupidity.

But human feelings are far more complex. Literature, the arts, and creativity in general all show the extraordinary capacity of human beings to create shared worlds. There is a high risk that mass participation in social networks won't lead to 'collective authorship', but to a swarm of totally

---

14   For a legal and historical overview of memory and the right to be forgotten in the digital age, see Viktor Mayer-Schönberger, *The Virtue of Forgetting in the Digital Age*, New Jersey: Princeton University Press, 2009.

superficial interactions. As Michel de Certeau argued it is time, and time only, which makes it possible to shape the everyday world 'below'. [15] When you do not have a place of your own and act on the territory of others; even if you cannot implement a long-term strategy, you can still resort to tactics. So in theory, personal time can be used to build up significant relationships, in other-directed contexts such as social networks, whose rules are not established by users themselves. But even the most sophisticated, subversion tactics in the use of social media tools very rarely result in genuine zones of experimentation. Almost always free time is reappropriated by the digital spaces and diverted towards profit generation. Hence, an increasing number of people, and that include technophiles, are beginning to understand that there is something fundamentally wrong with the current system. As artist Richard Foreman has puts it: 'we've been pounded into instantly-available pancakes, becoming the unpredictable but statistically critical synapses in the whole Gödel-to-Google net.' [16] For sure, speed is a two-sided sword. The illusion of immediate search results on request (Google) and of immediate sociality on demand (Facebook) reduces the depth of book culture and also the possibility to build up a signification-rich world. Richard Foreman asserts:

> But today, I see within us all (myself included) the replacement of complex inner density with a new kind of self-evolving under the pressure of information overload and the technology of the 'instantly available'. A new self that needs to contain less and less of an inner repertory of dense cultural inheritance — as we all become 'pancake people' — spread wide and thin as we connect with that vast network of information accessed by the mere touch of a button. [17]

Individual interiority empties itself here in order to completely pour itself again into the vessel of digital exteriority. This process is related to external stress, that is the permanent pursuit of significant responses (in terms of knowledge) and worthwhile contacts (in terms of affect) sought out by individuals. The networks' responses, as they are given by mechanical appliances (computers, cables, infrastructures) and content devices (software programs), belong to the scientific domain. But as Feyerabend notes where science wants to impose a single truth, it displays the quality of the religious. [18] As the mother of technical thought and technological objects, it is like a gas that saturates any discursive space, by imposing itself through the proselyting methods which have been invented and perfected by the world's most ancient and universal hierarchy: the Catholic Church. Just as a good shepherd takes good care of his flock, so does the modern technocrat cater for all the needs of his sheep, provided they are docile and transparent, sincerely declare all their concerns, and embrace the Gospel of digital society. What is new is that the sheep now need to actively self-define themselves according to the criteria that have been put at their disposal. They do not constitute an indistinct mass, yet their identities differ only minimally, and these variations are defined by very clearly specified criteria. That is the only way digital technologies can offer a personalized and immediate truth satisfying all the users' wishes at the same

---

15    Michel de Certeau, *The Practice of Everyday Life,* trans. Steven Rendall, Berkeley: University of
      California Press, 1984.
16    Richard Foreman, 'The Pancake People, or, the God's Are Pounding on My Head', *Edge*, 3 August 2005,
      http://edge.org/3rd_culture/foreman05/foreman05_index.html.
17    Foreman, 'The Pancake People'.
18    Paul Feyerabend, *Against Method. Outline of an Anarchist Theory of Knowledge*, 4th ed., New York:
      Verso Books, 2010.

time. Google, Facebook and the other lesser deities of the economy of search and attention, are therefore all minor hypostases through which we celebrate scientific religion and the rituals of emancipatory technology.

We are impatient to learn what the search algorithms have ferreted out for us. Even if we are in a hurry, and if a few seconds less or more appear of vital importance, we still remain in control. This is because the sociality provided by Google and Facebook has managed to make us acquire a phenomenal amount of self-control. We anxiously check out our email several times a day, we sometimes even maintain more than one mail account. We monitor our Facebook wall and keep watch over the feedback of our followers on Twitter. We make sure that we haven't missed any message on our smartphones, tablets and GSMs, all while we plug into Skype, MSN, or any other chat system. This is what turbo-capitalist sociality looks like and it forces us to control and compulsively retouch our digital profile in case we fall short of the 'world outside'. We verify that we exist because if we aren't here and there (and now), it is proof that we do not exist. 'Self-control' in its primary sense of 'controlling oneself' has become a second nature, an automatic reflex induced by the presence of technological objects through which we partake in a global technological system. We expect people to answer our mails, react to our posts, we want to be recognized, and 'tagged'. We want a lot of attention, but we get only crumbs and snippets of time, of the same quality as we can afford to give to others, who are like us far too busy, with the creation of a digital alter ego. Welcome to the performance society!

Despite being less codified than your run-of-the-mill religion, the superstitious rituals that accompany the daily use of digital tools is the seasoning for the tasteless fare online. Meanwhile, the control mechanisms put in place 'for our security' are militarizing all outdoor space and now are monitoring all online behavior too. As a consequence, the 'inner space' of Foreman's 'pancake people' is extremely circumscribed, as they live in fear of losing their 'friends', acquaintances, and followers. [19]

Techno-enthusiasts, would like us to believe that distracted-attention generated by the sheer number of web users can easily be converted into cash revenue. In the knowledge economy, the more people who bring in their own expertise, the greater the total amount of wealth generated. But it is not true that people today have more real knowledge. To know everything about a sitcom, celebrities, the latest fashion trend in Soho when you live in East Oslo, does not amount to knowing more or to a superior form of knowing. We do not become any wiser by keeping up-to-date with our digital 'friends' on Facebook or followers on Twitter. The sum of this knowledge only serves the purpose of accelerating digital processes. Raoul Vaneigem's ecstatic assertion, "say anything, nothing is sacred" is trivialized by the mass of banalities circulated on social networks. So everything become semi-sacred and semi-trivial, every utterance is 'equipollent' (equivalent in significant) because it appears as if nothing truly new can ever be said.

Yet not all knowledge is equal. Nor is all equivalent. It's true that my old aunt Margaret may never be able to handle a smartphone or a VoIP – though she might learn it if she received personal-

---

19    The idea, that inner space is the last space left to explore can be traced back at least to J.G. Ballard's guest editorial for New World Science. See J.G. Ballard, 'Which Way to Inner Space?', *New World Science Fiction*, vol. 40, Concrete Island, New York: Farrar, Straus and Giroux, 1998, pp. 116-118.

ized instructions. But she knows how to live in her world, which continues to be the real world for the largest part of the world's population, and also for us, even though we tend to forget it when seated in front of our screens. Is there so much of a difference between repairing a leaking tap at home, mending socks, or listening to a friend and learning how to post messages on one's Facebook wall? But why is it called a wall? Is it because it is an infinite space for graffiti? The two aforementioned types of skills might have a comparable degree of complexity, but both are very different. The first type makes individuals more autonomous, the second type is a form of knowledge-power that is entirely dependent on productions which are heteronomous (i.e. led by an other person's rules) vis-à-vis the world outside. This holds particularly true for those users who haven't got any clue about how Facebook works, technically speaking (and who therefore have zero autonomy with respect to the tool), even though they make compulsive use of it. When rules change, by virtue of 'default power', on Facebook, or on the platform I use to build up my identity, I become confused, and as a user get lost since what I have mastered has become useless knowledge which I now need to update. In a certain sense it's me that has become outdated and require an upgrade in this permanent education process where you learn strictly nothing save to know how to adapt to the system. When the organization of the personal account is altered by the service provider 'in order to enhance the user's experience', it is the identity itself which is shaken up. But how can we oppose the programmed obsolescence of expertise, if nothing that exists in the software really depends?

The very concept of opposition and critical attitude becomes obsolete, as well as the ability to seek alternatives. The articulation of thought is sucked away by the speed of change, the escape velocity required to flee the inconsistency of the sociality that is being created. In the next chapter we will see that this new sociality is part of a very explicit ideological project: anarcho-capitalist fundamentalism, a project that completely resonates with a vision of technology as liberation and salvation. The words used to represent users' online experience tell us all that we need to know about the hollowness of the myth of digital participation. 'I Like', 'FirstLink', 'Click Here', 'What Are You Thinking Right Now?' describe reactions which are not even bidirectional but only one-sided. On Facebook you can expresses your tastes, but criticism doesn't make any sense. The most common rejoinder being: 'well, if you don't like it, why you would you go there? Everything is online, so you're entirely free to choose what you like'.

But freedom is not the same thing as a free choice between black and white. Rather free choice is a constructive process, which, when undertaken without necessary nuances, leads to absurd simplifications. 'Voting' procedures may sometimes be implemented, e.g. on Amazon recommendations, or regarding the evaluation of Wikipedia entries. The pooling of these resources and their analysis is used to establish rankings that is to organize the results according to values expressed by users, which are bound to change over time. We will return to this in details later on, when talking about confidentiality and profiling. The evangelists of digital democracy will argue that online expression of preferences will deal with the 'dictatorship of the majority' issue once and for all. This problem is most apparent in what is the world's most widespread ranking system: Google's PageRank. In the beginning each and every link to a site was considered to be one single preference, or 'vote'. Therefore search results were those that 'had been vouched for by the majority'. But very early on these simple algorithms were contextually tweaked through the diktats of a global algorithm, TopRank, which is based on individual data profiling (earlier searches, browsing, history, locale, etc.). Here appears the ideology of a very specific kind of transparency, which can only be achieved by pilfering individuals' data on a grand scale, and throwing their inner life into the vortex of an online system. All these contents gathered through tracking procedures, are separated into smaller and smaller subsections enabling ever more finely preferences-atuned services and product for the individual web user.[20] Algorithms can semi-automatically extract an appropriate response to any request expressed by other users 'likes'.

The spatial metaphor of an 'inside' (individuality) vs. an 'outside' (collectivity, network) is useful in order to grasp the fatal error of the technological miracle, which is a distinguishing feature of the turbo-capitalist dystopia. The knowledge amassed in the 'outside', a.k.a. 'Big Data' is illusory, because whatever knowledge is useful to humans is not 'outside' and is also not easily transfer-able. Even though knowledge can be acquired, shared, exchanged, transferred, and rendered objective, it still remains based on a highly individual process of the imagination. Contrary to the unreflective total recall of digital devices, identity building is a process where we continually shed knowledge, and memory, in order to recreate it, just as our physical body is constantly regener-ated through cellular processes.

When we 'know' something or somebody, we clearly enter into a relationship with something that is external to our individuality. But not all relationships are equally interesting, and in need of deepening — and neither are all links on the internet. The dictatorship of 'zero cost' is worth exactly that — nothing.[21] The 'Like' culture has nothing to do with personal choices; it just rep-resents a pseudo-random judgment. Establishing a new connection is not easy. A network we navigate can be represented as a graph, composed of nodes and connected by arcs. The act of connecting nodes with a new arc is not trivial. In a graph with three nodes, {A->B->C}, if we trace an arrows from A to C, we change this small world: there is now a direct connection between the (formerly) first and last nodes. It is no longer necessary to pass through the second node, B. When nodes are people's profiles, as is the case in social networks, establishing a new con-nection (or cutting a previously existing connection) means also a change in power distribution. A direct line of communication means more autonomy than a line of communication necessarily passing through many others nodes. Therefore when we assert a new preference we split what was previously a continuum, and create new divisions of space.[22] This requires time, effort and attention. It requires awareness, because if we establish a link, i.e. a bridge, between two points in the network, and it is poorly designed, the link will collapse with the very first person attempting to use it. The cult of the link is exactly the opposite: immediatism rules: 'everything has been said before', 'it's all out there', 'everybody's here already — your "friends" are waiting', 'your competitors are watching, while your clients are waiting for you', etc. You need only to type the right url and

---

20   For a short presentation of how tracking research see: http://donttrack.us/.

21   When we get a hundred free SMS for recharging mobile phones, to be sent within the next twelve hours, we are faced with a communicative possibility that costs nothing and is worth nothing, neither to the sender nor to the recipient. An act of communication is of value only through the effort and time spent on it. Yet this perverse offer of free communication is so powerful that it can even make us feel guilty for not having taken the extraordinary opportunity to send hundred of text messages in a short burst.

22   Graph theory can easily be used to show how in the internet (considered as graph) a new link can completely reconfigure the network itself and is therefore an act of radical creation. For an introduction to the topic, see Albert-László Barabási, *Linked: The New Science of Networks*, New York: Perseus Book Groups, 2002.

you're there, 'just open an account on this or that social network, and you'll be among 'friends'. The party is out there, out there – it's the inner world that is boring.

We can now understand the full extent of Pierre Levy's slogan: 'No one knows everything, everyone knows something, all knowledge resides in networks).'[23] This is a very treacherous aphorism indeed, both on account of what it implies, and due to its consequences. Hence, it demands our full attention. The tripartite of 'no one', 'every one' and 'all' can be understood in terms of a pseudo-Hegelian dialectic. The overcoming of the limits of the individual (thesis: no one knows everything) is via a positive reassessment of global knowledge (antithesis: everyone knows something), to arrive at the synthesis of the complete inverse of the external world: all the knowledge is 'out there' (i.e. reality equals information). It sounds entirely reasonable: since everybody knows something, everyone just has to 'throw out' what he knows and this infinite wealth of knowledge is now 'out there'. Participating in the construction of shared worlds now seems so easy.

As we will soon see in detail, everything, 'out there', has been the creation of individual minds, who are able to socialize, and become a collective. The apparently harmless idea of hoarding knowledge 'out there' in order to exploit it belongs to the belief in information as such[24] Too bad that there exists no information 'as such', unless it is meta-category intended to wipe off, like a sponge, the complexity of communicative interactions. What is the substance of information? Intangible and ethereal, digital information needs heavy hard disks made up of metals, silica and rare earths as support. Engineering and industry are required to manufacture the circuits through which digital information flows around and electricity (obtained from coal, oil, nuclear fusion, the wind or the sun) is essential to making information available. Without extremely sophisticated data unbundling mechanisms, information would not at understandable to us at all. The digital world is not disembodied; it a is material world. On the other hand, no support is external to us. Knowledge cannot be separated from the human brains producing it. To put it in more technical terms: minds are co-extensive to bodies, and bodies are co-extensive to minds. It may be that, some day, non-human bodies will be able to display conscious mental abilities, but these will not be of a human variety.

Consequently, even if this type of external support (whether digital or otherwise) would exist for knowledge (it already exists for information but information is not self-conscious) it would not act in our collective interest. The concept of automatic sociality run by machines is an absurdity. Even without going deeper into the argument, we are able to state with certainty that data in general, and Big Data in particular, is devoid of intelligence. Quantity of information does not in itself generate sociality. The quantity of information generated by Big Data does not make it amenable to sociability. Big Data does not liberate or empower us, nor does it automatically make us autonomous and happy. Collective network intelligence is actually a reactionary dream of control. When the collective imagination, no longer reflects on itself, it crystallizes and produces oppressive institutions.[25] Institutions are of course necessary for social organizations, but they almost

---

23   Pierre Lévy, *Collective Intelligence,* New York: Basic Books, 1995.

24   Manuel Castells, *The Rise of The Network Society: The Information Age: Economy, Society and Culture,* Hoboken: John Wiley & Sons, 2000.

25   Cornelius Castoriadis, *The Imaginary Institution of Society,* trans. Kathleen Blamey, Cambridge: MIT Press, 1997.

always hide their historical origins. They do not operate for the good of people, but merely in order to perpetuate themselves and self-reproduce, draining the energy of individuals in the process. We can easily imagine that the institutions that will arise from the collective technological imagination will be even more inhumane than the ones we have already witnessed in history. Consider the example of digital control, that is digital policing: if it is always somehow possible to oppose human domination, how will it be possible to rebel against the 'external' machine that has been entrusted with the task to ensure the law is respected?[26] It is not by accident that institutions are step by step adopting the network model and transforming themselves into reticular organizations. In doing so, they unload the negative externalities onto the weak parts of the network, and manage to concentrate even more power in the process. When institutions don't even have a public remit, or a quasi-democratic facade, but are blatantly governed by anti-social principles, such as are anarcho-capitalist private enterprises like Facebook, it should be obvious that the social network being shaped is a trap.

In conclusion: in order to communicate the Self and one's own identity, the correct approach is not to have less rules and a smaller range of tools for everyone to use. On the contrary, it is to have more rules, and a greater range of tools, which need to be appropriate for a variety of specific situations, and differ according to the type of communication being used. Only then is it possible to imagine a greater autonomy, meaning the power to 'establish one's own rules'. Mass participation on Facebook only sets the stage for an illusory world where only 'friends' exist – and no enemies. Worse still, where the best way to keep one's 'friends' is not to go out and meet them, but to continually update your own profile in a downward spiral of toxic social network addiction.

## 1.07 — PUBLIC AND PRIVATE, ONTOLOGY AND IDENTITY

Is what is private also public? According to Facebook, everything private should tend towards becoming as public as possible. Public meaning of course managed by, published on, and made available through Facebook, a private enterprise. But the social networks to which an individual belong are not the same as her or his 'behavioral networks' (the people we meets often, but who are not 'friends' e.g. parents, children, relatives, neighbors, etc. They do not correspond with our online networks either. Danah Boyd's writing on social networks is a good starting point for clarification.[27] The fundamental issue always remains the same: a personal ontology being created within a collective context. This is how Mark Zuckerberg thinks about it:

'You have one identity,' he emphasized three times in a single interview with David Kirkpatrick in his book, *The Facebook Effect*: 'The days of you having a different image for your work friends or

---

26    Digital democracy based on the principle of a link per vote quickly turns into a system of retroactive recommendations (Google, Amazon, FaceBook) which effectively militarizes networks. Services that use profiling keep repeating: 'if you have nothing to hide, you have nothing to fear'. They argue that the law will not allow them use the information taken from the user to go against the user's own interests. This is a rather a hollow defense to hush up the truth that we have been completely robbed of our personal data.

27    See http://www.zephoria.org/ and Danah M. Boyd and Nicole B. Harison, 'Social Network Sites: Definition, History, and Scholarship', *Journal of Computer-Mediated Communications,* 13:1 (October 2007): 210-230.

co-workers and for the other people you know are probably coming to an end pretty quickly.' He adds: 'Having two identities for yourself is an example of a lack of integrity.'[28]

We at Ippolita have always posited that identity is a place of difference, for the biological, psychological, and cultural reasons we have already discussed.[29] With his moralism, Zuckerberg gives the impression he is about to cut through this Gordian knot of lies, by asserting the necessity of having one identity, clear and precise, in order to not deceive others. Zuckerberg would like us to believe that Facebook aims to reconstitute our identities, shattered in thousands fragments in our relentlessly competitive modern lives, and that he wants to give us back our lost (mythical) integrity. So he pushes us to form a personal profile, reconciling, as in an advertisement of ourselves: hard working, family oriented, a sexual subject, a spiritual person, a kind-hearted character and so on. Facebook as the platform for personalized mass self-marketing.

Eliminating identity is impossible just as it is impossible to abolish power. This is fortunate as it is what makes evolution, change, and communication possible. Identity should be managed, multiplied, altered, re-created — just like power needs to be. To communicate means to talk or write from out a specific place, that is to assume an identity, or to built up knowledge-power. Writing is based on language, language on identity, which in its turn is based on power. Therefore whichever means we use to communicate, we are already entangled in the construction of identities, both personal and collective.

But social life, as practiced today, flawed and perfectible as it may be, implies the possibility to circulate, at will, different versions of ourselves, resulting in different identities for others to mirror, leading us to adjust ourselves to new social relationships. We are not 'the same person' to each and everyone. So the question is not about being able to access various level of depths within a single individual profile, but to be really different according to the predominant situation. Despite this apparent incoherence, this is absolutely necessary and positive for us, in order to be in accordance with our own integrity. As we shall see later on in detail, it is important to spread knowledge-power, by strengthening the bonds with our loved ones, by establishing connections where there were none before, by cutting off the dead wood. What definitely should not be done is to solidify knowledge-power into a static identity by accumulating data that is only commercially relevant, and has the personalization of advertisements as its sole purpose.

In everyday life, we do not behave the same way in the presence of our parents as we do with our children. We don't talk with our children about our professional problems, unless for some reason, we to make them feel they bear some responsibility for them. If we discuss the same subjects with our friends, we would still do so in a different manner. We do not go partying with our parents, and certainly not with the postman. We don't have sex with our boss either (or at least not generally). So why should he be our 'friend' on Facebook or, worse still, share the same confidential information that we share with our partner? Yet, the emotional bonds with members of our own family is no less important than the affection we feel towards our friends.

---

28    David Kirkpatrick, *The Facebook Effect,* New York: Simon & Schuster, 2009.
29    For a radical approach on identity as place of difference, see: Rosi Braidotti, *Metamorphoses: Towards a Materialist Theory of Becoming,* Cambridge: Polity Press, 2002.

We probably spend most probably more time at work than our love life. This is simply because we have are faced with different types of relationships, within different social networks, each demanding a different identity.

Also we should consider the constantly evolving nature of identity. Rebelling against parents is commonplace for a fifteen year old, but at thirty this impulse makes no sense – and if still does persist, is likely the symptom of developmental problems. Our friends from primary school, the few we haven't lost of sight altogether (only to find them back on Facebook of course) remember a very different person. Similarly, our first love may in retrospect see us as a ray of sunshine in their lives, while our ex-partner detests us because of the alimony that has to be wired every month. We repay in kind by showing only coldness and contempt; love is over, things have changed. As we change our social relations express the changes that makes us alive. We will list several examples to show the perversity of the mechanisms of fixed identity that are promoted, or rather imposed, by Facebook. These examples, admittedly slightly stylized, and set in the feminine gender, are unfortunately quickly becoming, or have already become a reality.

Example 1, Dismissal: A very competent young female teacher, adored by her students, is filmed drunk at a party among friends. Explicit pics and clips are circulating in no time on Facebook, posted and reposted by 'friends' of 'friends' until they finally reach her director and the college's board. The teacher is now no longer allowed to apply for her tenure, and is severely reprimand. Her plea that her private life has nothing to do with her work as teacher is dismissed, and she is fired for being a bad example to her students.

Example 2, Violence: A mother tries to protect her child against her violent husband, is beaten, and violated. After a horrific ordeal she finally manages to escape her tormentor. She moves to another, remote city and starts her life over with her son. The nightmare is over. But then there is Facebook. Her ex-husband out where she is simply by reading her messages, and by checking out an app she occasionally uses, which gives away the user's exact geolocation. In order to regain a private life she will have to close her account. In her case, merely being active on Facebook can put her life in danger.

Example 3, Suicide: A young woman is caught on video by 'friends' while she is fellating her boyfriend in the college toilet. The clip is instantly on line, and in no time everyone knows about her private, but now very public skills, which are extensively commented on Facebook. She tries to defend herself, switches educational institution, but to no avail: her new friends are also on Facebook, and know 'what kind of girl she is', She is constantly ridiculed, insulted and marginalized. 'You did it, so now you get what you deserve' is the attitude openly expressed which convinces her life is no longer worth living. She slashes her veins in her bathtub after having written one final message on her Facebook wall. [30]

---

30  There have been a number of 'Facebook suicides' documented throughout the world. See http://www. repubblica.it/2008/08/sezioni/cronaca/suicida/suicida/suicida.html.

## 1.08 — PRIVACY NO MORE: THE IDEOLOGY OF RADICAL TRANSPARENCY

In its first five years of 'public' existence, (2005-2010) Facebook, has increasingly narrowed the private space of its users. [31] Facebook centers its public relations drive around transparency, or even, radical transparency: 'our transparency with regard to machines shall make us free'. [32] We have already deconstructed the assertion that 'you cannot be on Facebook without being your authentic self'. [33] The 'authentic self', however, is a tricky concept. Authenticity is a process where you become yourself with others, who in their turn, contribute to one's personal development. It is not an established fact, fixed once and for all.

But the 'faith' in Facebook is a blind faith, an applied religion, impervious to reason. Members of Facebook's radical transparency camp, Zuckerberg included, believe greater visibility makes us become better people. Some claim, for example, that because of Facebook, young people today have a harder time cheating on their boyfriends or girlfriends. They also say that more transparency should make for a more tolerant society in which people eventually accept that everybody sometimes does bad or embarrassing things. The assumption that transparency is inevitable was reflected in the launch of the News Feed in September 2006. It treated all of your behavior identically... [34]

The fact that 'behavioral' social networks and 'affinity' ones are merged together online, is, as we have seen before, the cause of serious problems in daily life. Yet the merger is one of the main dogmas of Facebook, and for very specific, commercial motives: in order to maximize the sale of online advertisements, it is necessary that users' data are in the open as much as possible, and that their privacy shrinks to the point of being only a outdated notion from the past. Advertisers must be able to verify, without infringing on anyone's privacy, that their ads have indeed reached the Facebook pages of those users whose profiles match the hypothetical consumer of their product or service.

All this of course is 'for our own good'. This at least is Facebook's official stance, a mission the company broadcasts by way of numerous press releases, interviews and road shows. But what if I do not want to be totally transparent? Not because I have something to hide, but simply because I don't want everybody to know the same things about me at the same time. I have many aspects, I am not afraid of contradictions, and I have more resources than my Facebook account allows me to express. I like to introduce chaos and discordance in the data that purports to define me, I like to shake up the deck.

Or, more simply: if I don't want to go out with you tonight, I should be able to tell you I'm tired, and that's it. I don't want you to feel hurt, or worse still, feel betrayed when you find you discover, on a mutual friend's Facebook wall that I wasn't at home the previous night, but had actually had gone to a party with other friends. Social life is far more complex than radical transparency is able to anticipate, unless we give up a large part of us that makes us different from others, and

---

31   See Matt McKeon's interactive graph, 'The Evolution of Privacy on Facebook', http://mattmckeon.com/facebook-privacy/.

32   Danah Boyd, *Facebook and Radical Transparency (a rant)*, 14 May 2010, http://www.zephoria.org/.thoughts/archives/2010/05/14/Facebook-and-radical-transparency-a-rant.html.

33   David Kirkpatrick, *The Facebook Effect*, p. 210.

34   David Kirkpatrick, *The Facebook Effect*, pp. 210-211.

therefore more us interesting and desirable to others. Otherwise we risk simply become lost in a group where we all hold the same opinion on all things.

The personal data of social networks, such as Facebook, is stored in the cloud, not under out watchful eye like the private diaries of the past. Not so long ago, account holders could not even delete their Facebook entries, which instantly became the 'non exclusive property' of the firm, in order for this data to be sold to third parties. Of course, nobody was talking about copyright here. Sure, Facebook does not intend to make money with our low-resolution holiday photos nor with our hastily posted messages. The average user is not an artist ripe for exploitation. However, data mining made for profiling purposes, all this material accumulating in data centers, i.e. Big Data, constitute a serious problem. [35] Nothing is free, especially not in Web 2.0, where the price to be paid for the 'free service' ('It's free and always will be' proclaims Facebook's start page) is to consent to the retrieval, indexing, and exploitation of all the data in the users' profiles, and especially of mutual relations.

But what about privacy? Online sociality is based on the absence of the privacy, meaning on the ability to mine emails, pictures, blogs, texts, etc.: to extrapolate key and propagate contextual and personalized advertisements. All this data is obtained from exchanges that are usually deemed to be 'private and confidential'. Google, Facebook and all social networks in general demonstrate the existence of spheres which are neither public nor private, and which are managed by technocrats, and more particularly by technocrats employed by private companies fueled by the profit motive. Privacy, literally, is the right to be left alone. For this reason, speaking of privacy in a collective, but privately-owned social network is an oxymoron, since the prime objective of a network is the circulation of information. When the information consists of the identities of the people making up the network, the idea to stay out (while being part of it) is a not an option. The only way to retain privacy is to not connect at all.

Privacy is a chimera: it only comes becomes apparent when we realize it has been violated. Ever since the Echelon scandal, everybody knows that privacy doesn't exist any more – and has not existed for a long time. [36] Yet, the problem with surveillance is not so much the disappearance of privacy, but the fact that the ensuing control and monitoring extends for such a long period of time. Each user has a digital 'finger print', a unique and personal identity-marker. Being part of a network means to be connected and to leave traces of our passage. It is the same case with phones: even if I get rid of my previous mobile, I am most likely to call the same people with my new phone as with my old one, and therefore, to reconstruct my social network. If a users profile exists that looks like exactly the same, identification is automatic and immediate: it can only be me. The way social networks function makes this even more disturbing, because the names of

---

35  The popular term *data mining* is vague and non-technical. Data analysis on the basis of half-automated systems is a vast and heterogeneous research field. To simplify, we can say that generally *data mining* is not focused on the identification of real people, but the extraction of significant correlations in large amounts of data through algorithms, e.g. interesting patterns in groups of aggregated data (*cluster analysis*), or data out of the norm (*anomaly detection*). *Data mining* becomes problematic when the goal is to profile users for surveillance purposes – this is the specific use of data mining we are referring to here.

36  Duncan Capbell, *Électronique Planétaire,* Paris: Editions Allia, 2001.

members of a group are generally not hidden to non-members, so as not to limit the possibility of non-members to join the group. It is not difficult to generate identifiers, or trace-marks, at the group level, e.g. a list of all the Facebook groups to which an individual user belongs.

Supporting the free flow of information has nothing to do with this type of 'sharing' everything and anything in an automated and mandatory fashion. This is not the sharing of Copyleft i.e. sharing knowledge, free of patent laws, trademarks and non-disclosure agreements. Facebook's type of 'sharing' is not about making knowledge available in the public domain. 'Publishing' on Facebook, does not make information public, but enables information to be managed by a private company, i.e. Facebook. [37]

There are several ongoing studies on systems of mass de-anonymizing and re-identification, using specifically devised algorithms on social networks. All that is required is a map of a small social network (relations between nodes must be known) in order to use that information to re-identify (by their real names') the users of a larger network. For example, knowing the set of relationships between a group of Flickr users, and then charting the segment of them who also maintain an account on Facebook, enables de-anonymization of a large number of profiles on the wider network. [38]

There are also other methods, which are simpler and just as effective, that demand less mathematical knowledge. Knowledge of website building and malicious code writing allow de-anonymization through browser history stealing and profile hijacking. Our personal or collective fingerprint trail can easily by tracked down through the data collected by the search engines we make use of, especially if we never clear our browser history and keep cookies and the logins active all the time. To get hold of this data, bait-sites are setup to lure in users with the promise of winning free gifts or pornography. The hidden code, java script or something similar, downloads and records browser history, cookies, passwords, software used, keystrokes and then cross-checks all the data obtained. The process of de-anonymization is even easier with the help of LSO (Local Shared Object) a kind of flash supercookie, which cannot normally be deleted by the web browser. [39]

The socialbots, discussed earlier, were studied in a recent experiment by Vancouver University researchers, which demonstrated the limited security of social networks. [40] Users, have the tendency to increasingly 'mechanize' their online behavior and it becomes easier to emulate their activities through bots. This makes social networks vulnerable to infiltration by bots that spread

37   See the afterword of Ippolita, *The Dark Side of Google*.

38   Arvind Narayanam and Vitaly Shmatikov, 'De-anonymizing Social Networks,' *Proceedings of the 2009 30th IEEE Symposium on Security and Privacy*, pp. 173-187, http://www.computer.org/csdl/proceedings/sp/2009/3633/00/3633a173-abs.html.

39   On Supercookies LSO see: http://www.wired.com/epicenter/2009/08/you-deleted-your-cookies-think-again/. The Mozilla 'Better Privacy' add-on is still an effective tool against LSO's (but not profiling). https://addons.mozilla.org/en-US/firefox/addon/betterprivacy/.

40   Yazan Boshmaf, Ildar Muslukhov, Konstantin Beznosov, and Matei Ripeanu, 'The Socialbot Network: When Bots Socialize for Fame and Money', *Proceedings of the 27th Annual Computer Security Applications Conference (ACSAC'11)*, December 2011, http://lersse-dl.ece.ubc.ca/record/264/files/ACSAC_2011.pdf.

disinformation and propaganda. The larger the infiltrated network is, the more effective the campaign of disinformation. The Canadian researchers' experiment shows how social bots mimic the
behavior of real users. First they create fake profiles and start sending 'friend requests', respond-
ing adaptively to the reactions of real users. Within eight weeks, the socialbots had managed to
infiltrate 80% of the targets, depending on the users privacy settings, and implanted themselves
permanently as nodes in an online network of trust. When a socialbot has got the trust of a web
user it can get access to private data, just like a human being. In this sense, our information is
even more vulnerable than if access was completely public since other users are convinced that
programs are 'friends' and not some malicious codes designed to steal their data. This research
proves, if such a proof were ever needed, that Facebook's much vaunted 'immunity' security
systems are inadequate in preventing large-scale malicious infiltration.

According to Zuckerberg, improvements are constantly made in order to enhance users' online
security, but these do not solve the decisive problem: user identity, understood in this context as
authenticity. In order to trust a friend, whether online or offline, it is first necessary to ensure that
she really is who she claims to be, that is to authenticate her identity. But, for the time being, users
of social networks do not manage the authenticity of their own identity. This verification is done
for them by algorithmic systems, run by for-profit firms which offer these social networking services for free. In this way we arrive at the somewhat paradoxical situation that in order to 'access
ourselves', that is to access our emails, Facebook pages, Twitter account, etc. we have prove who
we are through logins and questions. Distributed authentication systems, as used by Facebook
Connect, Google Friend Connect, or OpenID have a tendency to shift the authentication problem
to third parties. Are you who you claim to be is the question an online service we are accessing for
the first time will ask. Please click here and let us check out your data on your Facebook profile,
where, as is generally assumed, you only tell the truth. To authenticate oneself hence means to
deliver authenticity, meaning literally, to ensure that 'the same' (autos) is 'authoritative' and that
this authority comes from the inner 'me' (entos < intus), and not from some third person outside.
In other words: autos-entos (me, myself), is the authority for me, myself. I have created my own
identity and I am managing it myself. This of course entails that I am able to give a meaning to my
identity and that I am able to communicate that meaning in an intelligible manner. Which in turn
necessitates that users are both autonomous, and competent in handling digital instruments. In
practice it should be enough for online services which I am accessing through search engines to
stamp (earmark) my entry, without capturing data that has the sole purpose of profiling. Think of
the stamp you get at a music venue, without the organizers asking audience members for their ID
cards, demanding to know who their friends are, or inquiring about their tastes and relationship
status, in short, all the information available to the service providers which manage our online
identities.

The correct ideological position here would be to protect the authentication process itself. This is
far too important an issue to be left in someone else's hands, such as machines, institution, companies, which all have ulterior interests in profiling users instead of simply checking our identity
and securing our browsing. These companies all act in the expectation of being able to sell our
data on to the highest bidder in case we would represent any kind of interesting prospect, for the
police, an intelligence service, or an authoritarian government. In the name of radical transparency, we are consenting to increasingly accurate profiling and contributing to the vast pool of
data which social engineers have at their fingertips.

## 1.09 — FREE MARKETS AND FINANCIAL BUBBLES

The radical transparency of Facebook users finds no equivalent in the firm's own financial deal-ings, which are singularly opaque and openly disregard the rules of the market economy. This dangerous game has resulted in developments heralding an even larger speculative bubble than the 'dot-com' boom at the start of the Millennium. In our discussion we will knowingly use only pro-market sources, such as the Wall Street Journal and the Financial Times.

Here is a story that almost beggars belief. On January 3, 2011, Goldman Sachs together with the Russian company Digital Sky Technologies (DST), is in the process of investing $500m in Face-book, while giving its richest clients the opportunity to invest in their turn. [41] Note that Goldman Sachs are, as risk assessors one of the firms which are among the main actors responsible for the financial crisis. The Security and Exchange Commission (SEC), the body that is supposed to supervise the financial markets, goes on alert: one of the few rules it enforces is a limit of 500 separate investors in off-exchange deals, above that number a company is obliged to list publicly, i.e. on Wall Street. In order to enter an IPO (initial Public Offering) companies need to make their accounts public, to enable investors and potential shareholders to arrive at an informed business decision. Goldman Sachs' route around this 'obstacle' was to create a special vehicle for a few selected über-rich clients, while making $1,7bn profit in the process. This clearly transgresses the rules of the market, enabling Facebook's shares to continue being traded on the secondary market, and therefore avoid the need to make the firm's balance sheet public.

Curiously, the firm's valuation is multiplied in the next twelve month by a factor five, and then doubled again in the following half-year: at the end of 2009. Facebook was valued at $10 billion, rising to $25bn in July 2010, and to a further $33bn in August. There were rumors of $50bn figure by the end of December 2010. [42] Meanwhile, post-dotcom Google's valuation was $23bn in August 2004 (when it IPO'ed), but Google is at least an innovative tech firm, whereas Facebook merely offers a mash-up of already existing technologies. On January 20, 2011, it was announced that the Facebook IPO won't happen after all, as Goldman Sachs got cold feet at the prospect of a clash with the SEC. American small investors were furious they could not get in on the deal, while über-rich speculators who went onboard with Goldman Sachs' offer were laughing all the way to the bank with the promise of lucrative profits. [43]

Facebook manages to skirt even the most minimal of financial controls. The firm's valuation is val-ued at more than six times its gross revenues (only two times for Google), and it has accumulated half a billion dollars in cash so it can finance new investments. The fact is that Goldman Sachs was able to finance Facebook out of its own debts (just six months before investing, Goldman Sachs had to fork out $550m on settling a case of fraudulent misconduct), through luring inves-

---

41   Peter Lattman, 'Why Facebook Is Such a Crucial Friend for Goldman', *New York Times,* 3 January 2011,
     http://dealbook.nytimes.com/2011/01/03/why-Facebook-is-such-an-important-friend-for-goldman-
     sachs/.

42   Joseph Menn, Francesco Guerrera and Shannon Bond, 'Goldman Deal Values Facebook at $50bn',
     *Financial Times,* 4 January 2011, http://www.ft.com/cms/s/0/e0dad322-173c-11e0-badd-
     00144feabdc0.html#axzz1KzW89fTA.

43   Anupreeta Das, Robert Frank and Liz Rappaport, 'Facebook Flop Riles Goldman Clients', *The Wallstreet
     Journal,* 19 January 2011, http://online.wsj.com/article/SB1000142405274870395400457609044004
     8416766.html#articleTabs%3Darticle.

tors with a prospective IPO of Facebook. [44] When Facebook finally came to Wall Street, it was valued at $115bn. A great bargain for those early investors, who are bound to cash in big time, but it is less likely to be lucrative for the small investors, as these astronomical valuations are causing a financial bubble of enormous proportions. Early financing for Twitter, Groupon, and all other technological start-ups was a matter of millions, not billions of Dollars. Yet all the same, the mechanisms which made it possible to yield colossal profits from 2.0 start-ups' IPOs have began showing serious structural strains. This is well illustrated in the analysis of post-IPO transactions in LinkedIn (May 2011) and Groupon (November 2012) shares, which we take as early signs of the impending collapse of Facebook. The two aforementioned firms were something of a success on the stock exchange, especially Groupon, which had carried out the most important financial operation in the technology sector since Google's IPO in 2004. But soon after the 180 days anti-speculation delay before which trades were not allowed, LinkedIn share prices plummeted. Meanwhile, Groupon's devaluation had started immediately after the IPO, as if the boom-bust (or creation-evaluation-investment-profit-taking) cycle had suddenly accelerated yet again.

Obviously, these firms do not rely on artificially inflated profits alone they are totally dependent on exploiting the data they have accumulated from their users. As a consequence, investors have started to have second thoughts about these firms' growth potential. As we have learned from the ongoing financial crisis, the growth perspective is all what matters. This irrational system is now continuing its course full throttle, driven by the law of data. We live in a data driven society, with our economy and financial markets manipulated in real time through technical systems of control based on the pool of available data. Therefore, there are more and more opinion polls, a plethora of measurements are carried out, as if to factor in what cannot be quantified: the social well-being, which is a function of individual well-being. The impact of profiling system on individuals is even more difficult to evaluate.

There are cases where the obsession with metrics and data starts becomes counter-productive. Consider the example of Zynga, the global leader of online games. A company enamored with metrics, e.g. calculating the best predictive work performance creates an oppressive environment where wellbeing becomes impossible. In other words, if the law of machines is faster, more powerful, more data when these same demands are imposed on human beings, creativity withers and anxiety reigns. [45] Even the financial industry has become wary of the over-competitive atmosphere of corporations, as they see gifted workers suffering from psychological burnout. Zynga's IPO in December 2011 was an initial success but shares started depreciating the very same day. In Zynga's case, profits are dependent upon its ability to relentlessly churn out successful games, beating previous sale records each time. But it's a bit difficult to break records when you're already the top of your industry. As everybody knows, work does not set free and even less so in Silicon Valley.

It remains difficult to understand how Web 2.0 firms are evaluated in terms of worth and profitability. But we can understand a little more with simple arithmetic. Let us assume that Facebook's value in January 2011 was indeed $50 bn. At that time Facebook claimed 500 million users.

---

44   'The Goldman Sachs Facebook Deal: Is This Business as Usual?', *Public Policy*, 19 January 2011, http://knowledge.wharton.upenn.edu/article/the-goldman-sachs-facebook-deal-is-this-business-as-usual/.

45   John Cook, 'Is Zynga's Culture Really Rotten at the Core? Hear how Mark Pincus Described the Mission in April', *Geekwire*, 28 November 2011, http://www.geekwire.com/2011/zyngas-culture-rotten-core/.

$50bn divided by 500 millions equals $100, i.e. every Facebook account is worth $100. If I were a wealthy investor on Goldman Sachs' client list who'd bet, let's say, $50m (and has thus become 0.1% owner of Facebook), I would just pay someone to create new accounts. Create 1000 accounts – with a lot of links and entries (easy to do with customized software doing it automatically), at the rate of $100 for each account created, I make 100,000. I spend $50 on each account for 'the work' and gain $100 in return. In case there are any rich investors among our readers, please contact us since we know how to automatically generate hundreds of Facebook accounts and would gladly accept some of that money being created out of nothing! This is actually the underlying message of so-called 'abundance capitalism': everybody's going to get rich without doing anything, since the machines will do all the work for us. But for the time being the machines are betting on the stock exchange, using sophisticated algorithms, within an increasingly competitive and aggressive cultural environment while inflicting ever increasing workloads on humans, the latter have turned into a vast biomass for data extraction (users), or into mere producers-controllers for robots amassed in sweatshops. Little consideration is given to the disastrous consequences this has on individuals' lives. It has been proven that the cult of chance which is characteristic of the stock exchange, enhances a positive assessment of risk-taking and in this sense encourages irresponsible or even criminal behavior.

## 1.10 — FREE CHOICE AND THE OPT-OUT CULTURE

Social network gurus have a lot in common with financial traders. They are young, greedy, reckless, white, male and have difficulties forming relationships. We will talk in detail about nerd supremacy later on. For the time being, let's simply state that uncritically accepting Zuckerberg's positions, as a cure to social problems is equivalent to trusting a dentist with rotting teeth. Even if he is a great expert he is apparently careless enough to neglect his own health. Let us not forget that the good shepherd here is more interested in the data we are supplying than in our own well-being. Ultimately, the idea of radical transparency is put forth as the automated solution to remedy our inability to manage personal relationships. Like every commercial digital platform, it provides users with exciting new features that make the analog world seem poor in comparison. It is impossible for Facebook outsiders to have thousands of friends and stay in touch with all of them.

Speaking of 'free choice', there is a corollary to the default power that is worth noting: the 'opt-out' culture. Facebook alters the settings of millions of users without notification, providing only obscure references well after the fact. In doing this Facebook assumes that users themselves have no clue about what they really want, or at least, that their service provider knows better than the users do themselves. Digital social networks accumulate enormous amounts of user data and know how to monetize these with increasing efficacy thanks to feedback systems (votes, likes, report abuse etc.). Facebook retain the real identity of their users and have a more encompassing view of them than they possibly could have of themselves. Seen from their perspective it is logical to think that any change will be of benefit to them, since the data proves it in an unequivocal way. Later, the users can always decide to opt out and reject this new update. The assumption that new versions are always better is easy to grasp, in this sense innovations become self-imposing. Yet this issue is a very uncomfortable one, since, technically speaking, it is increasingly difficult to enable so many millions of users to choose easily what should be shared, and how to share it. Obviously the commercial social networks are not solely responsible for offering unwieldy privacy settings. Also for users, the 'optimal' strategy in the data-driven world of radical transparency, is to leave privacy settings more or less at the mercy of default power. Delegation is intrinsic to these tools. Users are attracted by their simplicity, but explicitly prefer to choose their own levels of sharing and exposure. In the same way, also from the point of view of the social media company, it is not easy to be user-friendly, capture a mass audience, and explicitly ask for user consent. Both for users and service providers, to operate by an 'opt-in logic' is more difficult and cumbersome than just delegating the choice to an algorithm. Of course, delegation is easier than self-management. Freedom of choice and autonomy are always difficult and risky. At a mass scale, it is impossible. Also, as we see in the 'Google culture', a celebration of the cult of innovation, permanent research and development, resulting in new software usually being released in untested, beta versions. True usability is only achieved after incorporating feedback from beta versions. Imposing a change that turns bad then becomes a manageable risk, since it can always be redressed if too many users start complaining.

Let's consider a real life scenario. From December 2010, Facebook began providing users with a facial recognition feature which automatically tags uploaded photos. Photos were scanned and faces identified based on images previously tagged in Zuckerberg's databases. When this software was introduced in the United States, it generated a large amount of controversy due to the threat it posed to privacy. Facebook's responded to criticism by suggesting users deactivate this feature by modifying their default privacy settings and opting out. Of course, when the new technology was released, Facebook neglected to tell its users (whether individuals or commercial partners) that the face recognition software had been activated by default on the social network. Facebook is not unique in this regard: Google, Microsoft, Apple, and the United States government have all been developing new automated facial recognition systems. The rationale given to the public is that this is 'for the good of users', and to protect citizens from dangerous terrorists. But the destructive potential of this technology is terrifying. In the worst case scenario, an authoritarian regime can semi-automatically 'tag' dissidents' faces captured in the streets by CCTV, create a comprehensive system of surveillance, and strike at the time it choses. In democratic societies, the technology is accessible to any tech savvy person. The logic of the Opt-out follows the same rule of developers: release early, release often (RERO). Constant updates allow user feedback to improve the software in successive beta versions. Yet, social relations cannot be quantified in these kind of logical cycles. The evaluative mistakes that are made when new technology is released can cause pernicious collateral damage.

Paradoxically, the webization of the social through mass profiling results in anti-social outcomes, since we all can become guilty by association or innocent by dissociation. Since human decision makers are increasingly delegating their power to algorithms, we can only expect an increasing number of evaluative errors of a kind that would be easily avoidable in real life, or within decentralized systems. To bear the same name as someone with a criminal record or listed as a terrorist by the federal police becomes a crime by association. The machines turn us into defendants because they are unable to distinguish us from someone who possesses the same name. If we have been victim of identity theft, and someone uses our credit card for an illegal activity, we also become culprits, insofar as our digital alter ego is guilty beyond doubt We are then no longer in a regime of 'innocent till proven guilty', but of 'guilty till proven innocent'. The criminalization of society is the logical outcome of profiling procedures – which ultimately derive from criminal profiling. In the end, there only obvious beneficiaries are the ill intentioned, who are always conscious of the need for an alibi.

Ordinary users are vulnerable to all kinds of abuse because due to the profiling which turn them into potential culprits. A Facebook account, or an account on Google+ or Twitter, is not owned by the user. It is a space made available to the user in exchange for letting herself be partitioned into commercially interesting bits and pieces. Strangely enough, the user herself carries zero value, since she must, prove who she actually is but also that she is innocent. In Facebook's case, there are a number of reasons for which users can be banned. The most common one is using a fake name. Some fake names are easy to notice, but not all are. 'Superman' is most likely an alias but which algorithm is sophisticated enough to make out whether 'Ondatje Malimbi' is truly a Kenyan user with a Swedish mother? To do so it would require access to civil registries, tax-office files and social security databases; a scenario which is actually not that unlikely. Incidentally, we should note that authoritarian governments appear to have far less reservations about implementing 'radical transparency'.

Managers of social media play a decisive role when it comes to what is permissible and what is not. In this sense they do help shape the rules of the society in which we live. They may not have the power to send somebody to prison but they actively cooperate with governments to enforce official and social laws of the land. Google specifically, since the beginning, has partnered with the American intelligence community. 'Google Earth' began as military cartography software developed by In-Q-Tel (a venture capital firm with CIA connections), and sold to Google in 2004. [46] After the USA Patriot Act was passed, with its harsh penalties for any collaborator who assists government enemies, commercial services providers have become extremely cautious. Enforcing censorship is less risky than hosting potential terrorists on their servers, or even people criticized by the US government. In countries under US embargo, dissidents' profiles are often closed while the regime's supporters are free to propagate their views on the government's controlled servers. While eulogizing Iran's 'Twitter Revolution', nobody, not even the people in the Administration – who waxed lyrical about its democratizing effect- seems to have noticed that Twitter was infringing the US embargo by offering its services to Iranian citizens... The PRISM case is nothing more than a mere confirmation of what we already know about Echelon, global tracking and global espionage, with the burden of the direct, automatic involvement of the major digital players. We can expect a lot of similar 'scandals' in the future.

Censorship is commonplace on Facebook, which often projects itself as guarantor of the net's neutrality, a concept we have already criticized. Facebook's very peculiar idea of democracy is based on its moralism, as we have seen at work before. Any user suspected of hate speech may be immediately banned. Here is a characteristic example:

My Facebook account has been cancelled, with that of ****'s because we were the administrators of the 'Against Daniela Santanchè' group (a far right Italian politician), or rather, I was administrator and **** the developer. I tried to log in but I only got a message that my account had been de-activated. I sent an email to the address I had found in the FAQ. At first I got no reply, but received the following response two weeks later, after a second message:

---

46   In-Q-Tel's core business is cryptography and surveillance in *cloud computing*. It would seem that the
     Pentagon has decided to make the *cloud* more 'secure', perhaps in order to avoid the embarrassment
     of another 'WikiLeaks' affair. See: Lena Groeger, 'SpyCloud: Intel Agencies Look to Keep Secrets in
     the Ether', *Wired*, 29 Jun 2011, http://www.wired.com/2011/06/spycloud-intel-agencies-look-to-keep-
     secrets-in-the-ether/.

Here is Facebook's automated response message:

Your account has been suspended as you are the administrator of a group that has been cancelled since it violated Facebook's rules on rights and obligations. Groups whose content or pictures promote the use of drugs, show nudity, allude to sexual acts, or attack an individual or a group of persons are not allowed. Unfortunately, due to technical and security reasons we cannot go into details about the group that has been cancelled. However, after having examined your situation, we have reactivated your account, which you now can access again. In order to avoid such situation again in the future, we advise you to check from time to time the content of the groups you are administering. If you do not want to carry out this responsibility, you can cancel your administrator status by clicking on 'Modify Member' on the group's main page, and then on 'Cancel Administrator' next to your name. For more information on unauthorized behavior on Facebook, please refer to the users' rules and obligations notice, which you can access by clicking on 'Conditions' at the bottom of every Facebook page. We thank you for your understanding.

– Users Organization Facebook Inc.

This user's account has been reactivated, but not that of the group's developer, probably because she was a repeat offenders had started other 'hate speech' groups. When were are in another house we behave according to their wishes: in this case we follow the behavioral rules of Facebook. It is peculiar that Facebook overtly bans pornography and corroborates the claim that it is a purveyor of emotional pornography. The emotional blackmail becomes explicit when users try to leave Facebook. The process of quitting Facebook is lengthy, users are required to reconfirm their intention to leave several times (it's easy to join, leaving is not!). Pictures tagging the user next to friends are displayed with a caption under each picture: 'you'll be dearly missed by so-and-so'!

The managers of a commercial service are not the only ones who decide what is hate speech. Your account could also be suspended due to blasphemy, for instance. Facebook is fluent in your language and able to identify offensive statements. Or some informer act as a guardian of public morality may have came forward and reported you. Nonetheless it easy to find racist, sexist, nationalistic and fundamentalist groups on Facebook, in which case it's up to you to help censorship and turn them in. Free choice and freedom of expression become tricky to defend when confronted with algorithmic logic, the same logic that makes Google, by default, withhold results it considers dangerous for you, meaning sites with obscene content. These hidden results almost always consist of display of explicit sex, which now makes up almost half of the world wide web, while explicit violence is largely acceptable. So if you wish to visualize all results you must de-activate 'Safe Search', the standard functionality has installed in default mode so as to protect you from yourself.

Racism, sexism, violence, nationalism, fanaticism, child porn, all existed before social media. Yet the ease with which these tools can be infiltrated by all the above is staggering, just as is the carelessness of people who trust machines to pass judgment on what is right and what not. The lack of a contextual framework for the flood of information on the net makes it a useful medium for spreading extremist, partisan or fraudulent content usually masquerading as appeals for a humanitarian cause or the defense of a common identity. Whether in our mailbox or through social networks, we are all familiar with the '419' type of fraud. The chain letters to assist a poor child who suffers from a rare disease, petition for noble causes, or the promise of wealth if we share our bank account with a rich Nigerian now in exile. The fact that such a message spreads through our circle of friends, lowers our defenses and allow it to be disseminated further without examination.

The case with malevolent, or ideological messages is more complex but follows the same principle. If you are invited by friends on the Facebook group 'United Against Poverty' chances are that you will 'Like' it, add a link on twitter and perhaps forward it to your mailing lists. Since we are accustomed to fragmented time and that our moments of full concentration are rather rare, we might not have noticed at first glance that the charity dinner meal was organized by an Italian neo-fascist group in support of Serbian enclaves in Kosovo. Unwittingly we may appear as sympathizers of the nationalist Bosnian Serbs, the far-right extremists who provoked genocide in Kosovo. Facebook, Twitter and Google's algorithms were all created by über-geeks who, with their limited experience of social issues should not be the ones make significant decisions on the role of technology in society.

## 1.11 — SUBSTITUTES FOR PRESENCE AND EMOTIONAL SOLACE

Many question remain on the issue of language, which we referred to as the second boundary of human and social experience. The algorithms of social network are in any case much less sophisticated than human language. The semantic web is still in its infancy and for the time being, it is up to the users to make themselves better understood by machines, which they do by diligently updating their digital profiles and simplifying their expressive richness to fit the 140 character limit of Twitter or the omnipresent 'like' button.

The first human boundary, the body, gets an even more brutal treatment. We must physically adapt to social media, by being instantly reactive, and learning a new digital mobility; the motility of our fingertips, so we can handle ever smaller keyboards and touch screens. It is the eye, however, which gains a more pivotal role because despite the promises of 'virtual reality', the screen still presents the sole access point to social media. Touch, taste, and smell are entirely absent (with the exception of console game where there is some tactile simulation). The rest of the senses are seldom used in the disconnected life too. Hearing has to cope with low fidelity sounds from mp3s to ringtones, which are worlds away from the quality of analog stereo. Yet what is expected from social media is always the contact with others, hence a physical contact, even if it has to be mediated. Seen in this light, all social media are a way to substitute for presence and make it possible to create a simulacrum which conceals absence and physical distance. They restore somewhat the otherwise fading memory of the other. Without social media, our daily life might become unbearable, now that we are used to being available at all times, while we procrastinate when we have to be physically in the present since we cannot be fully immersed in the screens and in the analog environment at the same time. Yet still, as Facebook has promised us, we feel that we take part in the creation of a new, shared world while comfortably seated in front of our computer without running the risk of confronting the dangers of the physical world.

Everything occurs faster in digital platforms, everything appears more real than reality and seems more intense. How can we be together with one hundred, or one thousand, 'friends', and interact with all of them? How can we follow all the updates about people, groups, companies, that we find interesting and influential? It is simply impossible. With Facebook, Twitter, and other social media, physical presence is substituted by sharing the platform prescribed by social media, and this prescribed sharing becomes the experience that shapes our everyday. Paradoxically, if you want to be more socially active, and to develop your digital self, you must become more passive in the physical sense. You must devote a lot of time to your profile in order to make it attractive and popular. You must practice for many hours everyday and commit yourself to interacting with smartphones and laptops. During all these hours spent on commercial networks the body becomes one big eye where we surf without being able to dive, hearing is hardly ever used, yet we are always ready to answer the suggestions coming from the reality 'outside'.

Real socializing then becomes more rare, but also more tedious and repetitive compared to digital sociality, where everything is both more abundant and fluid. It may even become more difficult to engage in socializing without the mediation of digital tools, since there are no 'friends' like on Facebook in reality, nor subscribers like on Twitter. A pseudo-presence keeps reality at a distance and even tends to substitute for reality itself. Tools increasingly monopolize the very demands they pretend to satisfy and rapidly become the only possible answer, irreplaceable and inevitable. [1] The logic of notifications push users to be at the mercy of the platform. If everyone travels by car it becomes quite dangerous to travel by foot, even if traffic is slow. If everybody communicates through cellphones, it will become difficult to find someone to chat to; the pedestrians you see in the street that are talking are talking to somebody else at the other end of an electro-magnetic spectrum. Ultimately, the real is less alluring than ever as we prefers to remain seated and use only our eyes with a remote control and keyboard, instead of getting up and going out to explore reality with the whole body and all its senses. There is an anthropological transformation taking place, which is governed by the media as they are able to make us forget that they are mere instruments of mediation; instead they have managed to come between our bodies and our perception of reality. Of course, teens and children seems to manage better than adult this situation, but make no mistake: they socialize thanks to the digital tools by staring at the screens together (this is one of the main differences from the typical adult individual use), only because the rest of their life is so controlled, planned, organized that paradoxically the commercial and private social networks are becoming their only space of 'freedom':

> The media would have us believe that they are means for accessing experiences, when in fact they have become portals which merely frame pre-scripted experiences as story-boards, and continually decode what is livable and accessible through the internet. [...] A cloning of life takes place, not in the sense that the media can replace experience, but in the sense that they are placed as necessary conditions of experience: they impose on us with the entice-

---

1    Ivan Illich remains an essential source on technological tools and the technical approach that underlies them, even if his analyses are somewhat dated by now. The distinction he makes between industrial tools and tools of conviviality remains very timely, however: 'I choose the term 'conviviality' to designate the opposite of industrial productivity. I intend it to mean autonomous and creative intercourse among persons, and the intercourse of persons with their environment; and this in contrast with the conditioned response of persons to the demands made upon them by others, and by a man-made environment. I consider conviviality to be individual freedom realized in personal interdependence and, as such, an intrinsic ethical value. I believe that, in any society, as conviviality is reduced below a certain level, no amount of industrial productivity can effectively satisfy the needs it creates among society's members.' See: Ivan Illich, *Tools for Conviviality* London: Fontana, 1975 (1973), p. 24.

ment of that old madam called Technology, whose trump card has always been her lascivious whisper 'I serve you'. [2]

So, what is the purpose of social media? We are happy to switch on our computer and to see all our Skype contacts. It is reassuring to have a lot of new messages in our inbox, and to find the stuff we have posted being commented on. Social media reassure us about the existence of a world outside and that we are truly part of that world. Every SMS, tweet and ringing of our mobile, do not have a merely communicative function, but they also, foremost, reassure use of our existence within a social network. The frenzied attention-distraction which is the outcome of social media usage is partially due to the fact that these technologies are relatively new. We are still learning how to deal with life in real time.

If we need constant reassurance, it is because we are all, to some extent, living in constant fear of being left behind and left alone. In a paradoxical way social media is a source of both comfort and frustration. We need to check all the time that we do indeed exist, especially in the social real, since we always run the risk that 'the others' are getting together without us, or that they are enjoying themselves somewhere else. To discover this in real time can be a blow to our self-esteem. Social psychologists talk about a pervasive apprehension that one is out of touch with social events and have labeled it FOMO (Fear Our Missing Out). [3] The experience of solitude has become as rare as silence, slowness and deep thinking. Perhaps after throwing everything about ourselves on digital platforms, to stay alone would mean to have to face an insufferable inner void and move around with a body whose connectivity 'limbs and senses' have been severed and in a sense disabled. The development of digital social media is a phenomenon that might be understood within a long-term process of dis-embodiment and increasing focus on sight at the expense of other body-senses, through the development of new media technologies. We do have a long history of distancing ourselves from reality and attempting to master it from the outside, through an all-powerful vision, while at the same time trying to be a part of it without getting hurt in the process. In a certain sense we have here, in a nutshell, the whole history of the technical system of the western world. But we will return to that aspect at length later on. Now we have considered the impact of social media on the physical body let us return to the role of digital sociality. The next section will investigate the political dimension of commercial social networks.

2    Franco La Cecla, *Sorrogati di presenza. Media e vita quotidiana,* Milan: Mondadori, 2006, p. 26.
3    John M. Grohol, 'FOMO Addiction: The Fear of Missing Out', *Psych Central,* 2013, http://psychcentral.
     com/blog/archives/2011/04/14/fomo-addiction-the-fear-of-missing-out/.

# PART II:
# THE LIBERTARIAN WORLD DOMINATION PROJECT:
HACKING, SOCIAL NETWORK(S), ACTIVISM AND INSTI-
TUTIONAL POLITICS

Everyone wants powerful friends. But they want friends more powerful than themselves.
– Elias Canetti, *Notes, Aphorisms, Fragments, 1973-1985*

### 2.01 — ONLINE IDEOLOGIES: THE ENLIGHTENMENT OF GOOGLE AND THE LIBERTARIANISM OF FACEBOOK

We are now coming to the issue concerns us most directly and is the closest to us: the political question. Even though politics appears to have very little connection with social networks, it is precisely the political ideology behind their respective business model that makes the major difference between the two giants of social media and long time competitors: Facebook and Google.

Ippolita has been active in critiquing the totalitarianism of Google, the platform that organizes all the world's information. Yet Google, in sense, can also be understood as a continuation of the Enlightenment project, the old dream of global knowledge accessible to all who benefit from its benign tyranny. To liberate the human being from her 'minority position' and let her gain autonomy was an aim of the Enlightenment, and we surely still appreciate this ideal. But if is true, the dark side of Google is also the Enlightenment's dark side: its unrestrained display of scientific rationality, technological progress and all of the myths associated with this. The regressive aspect of pure reason is the barbarity of total control, the alienation of the human, and of the life-world as a whole, which submits to the new religion of the machine. Google is undoubtedly the realization of the mega-machine in all its positive and negative aspects. Google develops innovative algorithms and filters to produce search results, which is ultimately the outcome of scientific research and technical invention. Yet Google's contents do not derive solely from profiling its users but also through the effort to create an abundance of free information. Access to information is managed by a technical subject, and not by the users themselves, who intend to be benevolent (the famous 'Don't be evil' motto), in the context of 'free market' capitalism.

In the United States, Google is perceived as politically 'liberal', which is tantamount to the center-left in European parlance. In the rest of the world, Google is perceived as supporting freedom of expression and to being opposed to repressive (and usually anti-American) governments. Google's disputes with China have earned it a reputation as a company standing for democratic values, or at least, democratic access to information. Free access to all information is good in principle. On the other hand, it can be understood as a new reinterpretation of the American Dream, only the frontier movement is now the conquest of digital information. Progress here is the accumulation of data, making the network denser, and, a universal vision of *koinè* (community, public,) on the global scale. Its involves an digital community which all contribute to the Encyclopedia and extends to searches, images, emails, books and all forms of information. So if we just gloss over the enormous problem that of all knowledge being managed by a private entity and large scale technocratic delegation, then, Google is not so bad after all. Of course, there will be an increasing number of conflicts due to Google's vast material interests, and the global reach of its services. These conflicts will include both private individuals and national and international authorities and involve infringements of the fundamental right to privacy, suspicion of abuse of its dominant market position, cartel-formation, collaboration with intelligence agencies, etc. But it is equally true that, as a company dealing with global knowledge, Google does not have a clearly definable political position.

The same cannot be said of Facebook, which is financially supported by the libertarian extreme right in the US — or to use that strangely apt oxymoron: the anarcho-capitalists. It is not easy to describe this particular ideology in a few sentences, especially from a European perspective. Libertarian ideas in Europe may come in many shades, from municipal libertarianism to anarcho-syndicalism, anarcho-communism, individualist anarchism, etc., yet they all are historically linked to anarchism, and therefore to socialist internationalism. From this perspective, a fundamentally anti-socialist reading of anarchism seems a logical absurdity.

Yet, as we shall see shortly, US rightwing libertarians not only play a central role in the everyday practices and corporate politics of Facebook, they are also prominent in shaping a whole set of values which has emerged over the past twenty years in the digital world. There are also significant connections between the world of hacking and libertarian ideas. From this vantage point, we are not out to explore the epistemic similarities between political philosophy and economic theory, as much as we are trying to uncover the governing principle linking apparently disparate phenomena like Facebook, WikiLeaks and Anonymous together.

## 2.02 — LIBERTARIANISM OR A SHORT HISTORY OF CAPITALISM ON STEROIDS
Libertarianism is comprised of a diverse group of political currents which came to prominence in the sixties, promoting a radical strengthening of individual liberties, in a strictly 'free market' context. These political positions have nothing in common with any kind of socialist tradition or practice. Some of its representative advocate keeping a bare minimum of shared society, and fall under the banner of *minarchism* proposing a minimalist state by deliberately confusing social relationships with social institutions. But truly radical individualism, posing as 'anarchist', as it is set out in the works of the better known libertarian authors such as Murray N. Rothbard, Robert Nozick or Ayn Rand, the founder of Objectivism, can only come to fruition if all oppressing social institutions are dismantled, including the State; hence the somewhat paradoxical definition of 'anarcho-liberalism' and 'anarcho-capitalism'. [4]

A good start to understanding the theoretical context of anarcho-capitalism, is in the work of Murray Rothbard, the first author to use the term in his writings. Rothbard, an economist who was also a student of Ludwig von Mises in New York in the 40s, created an original synthesis between the fierce anti-socialism of the Austrian School of economics and American individualist thinkers, especially Lysander Spooner and Benjamin Tucker. According to the Austrian School, free market capitalism is the only economic system that will vouchsafe individual freedom. It is good 'by nature' and therefore property rights are 'natural rights', and expanding property law is the only means to protect 'true liberty'. Any system interfering between the individual and the enjoyment of her private property is considered an oppressive tyranny which should be overcame by all means possible. Being a staunch

---

4    For an introduction to anarcho-capitalism with many references to the foundational texts see: http://www.ozarkia.net/bill/anarchism/faq.html.

advocate of individual freedom as a supreme good, Rothbard criticizes the moral legalism of those libertarians who accommodate the institutional status quo. For Rothbard market freedom can only be effective if the political practice itself is free of oppressive laws and regulatory measures by the State.

This approach fall shorts of the concept of liberty, since the only liberty that matters here, is that of the capitalist market, which is itself the outcome of the free agency of totally individuals motivated by their purely private interest in the accumulation of capital and consumerism. Since individualist anarchism is the political expression of individual liberty and the free market itself is the realization of that liberty; anarchism and capitalism are, according to Rothbard, one and the same thing. 'We are anarcho-capitalists. In other words, we believe that capitalism is the fullest expression of anarchism, and anarchism is the fullest expression of capitalism. Not only are they compatible, but you can't really have one without the other. True anarchism will be capitalism, and true capitalism will be anarchism.'[5]

Later on we will see the paradoxes underlying this blind faith in the benevolence of the free market. For now let us just emphasize how libertarian economic theory and policies are deeply related to the actual practices of Californian turbo-capitalism.[6] According to this line of thought individual liberty can only be realized through economic and monetary transactions. Considered as actors that are 'free by nature', individuals assign subjective values to the goods, services, and utilities available in an ideal free market system. Deregulation is the necessary condition to bring about a market that is 'benign by nature', without interference from the state and other public entities. Private property, as a 'natural right' is the foundation of individual identity; and the accumulation of goods and utilities constitutes the very substance of liberty.

Society from the anarcho-libertarian perspective is nothing more than the outcome of purely economic transactions at the individual level. In order to understand how such a vision has come into being we need to consider the historical context. According to Austrian economic theory, especially Ludwig von Mises, Rothbard's guru, the individual has a practice which defines her a priori, without need for her concrete actions to be taken into account. Through the study of this field, praxeology, we can arrive at fixed axioms.

Absolute truth derives from a single axiom only, the Fundamental Axiom or the principle of action.[7] The action axiom asserts individuals act in order to achieve their subjective ends, by applying means. This axiom is considered true for all human beings, at all times it can neither be denied nor falsified, since even negating this axiom is a form of acting. In philosophical terms, we may

5    'Exclusive Interview with Murray Rothbard', originally published in *The New Banner: A Fortnightly Libertarian Journal*, 25 February 1972, http://archive.lewrockwell.com/rothbard/rothbard103.html.

6    Conservative economist Edward Luttwak coined the term 'turbo-capitalism' in his book: *Turbo-Capitalism: Winners and Losers in the Global Economy*, New York: Harpers, 1999. We use the term in a much more polemic way, since it has become clear that today's economic trends have gone much further than Luttwalk's original analyses. See the second chapter of Ippolita's *The Dark Side of Google* ('The Googleplex, or Nimble Capitalism at Work'), where we draw a tentative description of Google's 'abundance capitalism' and of the 'Silicon Valley model' in general.

7    Murray N. Rothbard, 'Praxeology: The Methodology of Austrian Economics', *The Logic of Action One Method, Money, and the Austrian School*, Cheltenham: Elgar, 1997, pp. 58-77, https://mises.org/rothbard/praxeology.pdf.

describe the action axiom as a synthetic a priori proposition. From the fundamental axiom we can derive the following, equally unconditional truth: all individuals try to maximize their own utility. An individual always acts in such a way as to alter their present condition, which they perceive as unsatisfactory, in order to replace it by a condition deemed superior. Every human action therefore, consists in the elimination of a perceived want and of the satisfaction of a need. In other words, every human action tends towards the advancement of our own benefit. Every action is aimed at individual profit, but in an entirely subjective manner. The individual cannot avoid acting, moving and maximizing their own benefit and this is usually realized through the accretion of wealth. Plenty is good and more is even better.

The concept of time as a scarce resource sheds more light on the far-reaching influence of the doctrine of human beings as only truly free in the role of a consumer. This is precisely the definition of liberty underlying the digital social networks and 'Web 2.0' ideology. As time is a scarce resource, and all human action is oriented towards the satisfaction of needs through the consumption of goods, speed becomes the essence of achievement. On the basis of this purely deductive affirmation it follows that in the matter of production and consumption, the shorter the action lasts the better. Individuals, as consumers driven by subjective needs, prefer immediate gratification over long term satisfaction. Soon is good but the sooner the better. Speed above all else.

Naturally, praxeology as is has been developed in the writings of the Austrian School is more nuanced and complex is possible to present here. Yet, like any theory which presents it self as having absolute validity at all times and situations and for all people, praxeology exhibits a number of irreducible contradictions. Yet we need to consider one particular aspect it shares with the anarchist American individualistic tradition: absolute subjectivism. In classic economic theory, not only in English one (but also in Marx), there are objective values from which an axiology may be derived. [8] However according to Austrian praxeology no such thing as objective values exists. Economic exchanges can be beneficial to both parties, instead must be. If was this not the case then the axiom of profit maximization in as little time as possible would collapse. This entails that a good has a value that differs according to the individuals involved. Therefore, it is possible to gain distributed profits while at the same time underwriting unlimited growth, due to an errors in evaluating the wrongly estimated 'objective' value.

But this generalized expansion of individual economic welfare, which coincide with freedom tout court, is only possible in a situation of absolute economic freedom, without any interference by institutions. These institutions are by definition oppressive, as they seize private properties, manipulate conscious and dull the senses of individuals who are by nature able to strive for the satisfaction of their immediate needs. Hence, this is the absolute reference point of individualism: the individual, posited as an absolute subject, demands absolute freedom. She needs to be liberated, in the most literal sense, from all constraints.

---

8    An asset has a defined value that may be calculated in objective terms. In order for economic growth to develop in a capitalist system there must necessarily be winners and losers in any given transaction. In the ideal situation, where there is an exchange between two agents, if the good is worth ten units and is being bought for eleven, the buyer will be the loser; if nine units are paid for the same good, then it is the seller who loses out. From this transaction we are able to conceptualize and calculate profit, surplus values and so on.

The nation state, whether it is in a capitalist or socialist guise, is clearly the common enemy of the Austrian School and American individualism. All the more so since the Federal Government and all its institutions which claim to regulate the capitalist marketplace are effectively reducing individual freedom. Yet not all libertarians are in agreement about the absolute necessity to abolish the state. Nowadays, the most well known exponent of anarcho-capitalism is David Friedman, a US economist who favors a more gradual abolition of the state.

The whole anarcho-capitalist discourse can be encapsulated in one single word: privatization. Privatization can and should be extended to all sectors of society from firms to common law. If the individual is to triumph, no mediation whatsoever should be tolerated. But who then is this alleged individual? Our critique of digital social networks equally applies to anarcho-capitalism: the crucial question remains the relationship between individual and collective identity. Since humans develop their individuality within a social context it does not make sense, even theoretically, to consider the individual as a given, absolute identity separate from her social, biological, and cultural environment.

To be more specific: philosophically speaking, absolute subjectivism, from which the economic theory linked to anarchist individualism is deducted, is in open opposition with the radical relativism which characterizes of our research. Our ambition is not to describe social network 'as they really are', following the approach of technological determinism which apparently reveals a technology's true essence. Still less can we accept the idea that it would be possible for someone to really know everything about human nature, and hence to be able to infallibly deduce the essence of society as a whole. This would be unrealistic as well as unfair. The fact that there are 'realities' external to ourselves does in way mean that we can depend upon the 'the world' to demonstrate the truth of our beliefs. Some descriptions of the world are more appropriate than others, but only because they enable us to act better, not because they represent the world better than other descriptions. Radical relativism does not mean that all viewpoints are equally valid. On the contrary radical relativists support a position that strongly reflects their own particular standpoint on issues, precisely because there is no foundation or an ultimate, inherent truth.[9]

Additionally we may consider the very idea of a subject that is totally free from any link with the outside world and whose sole purpose is to act as rapidly as possible in pursuit of purely economic interests does not reflect the concrete experience of human beings and living beings in general. On the contrary, we constantly create and maintain links and relationships for no apparent economic reason at all. We do not always act to maximize our personal utility. We even sometimes prefer to postpone (or even to deny) the satisfaction of a personal desire not only to please other people, but even simply to expand our sense of freewill, in a complex game of weighing

---

9    According to constructivist theory it is impossible to give an objective description of reality since we live in a world build up from experiences, which themselves are the result of our constructed behavior. Cognition is a vital process, in a sense living is a cognitive process. Epistemological (pertaining to knowledge) issues are without doubt ontological issues (i.e. they pertain to the (life) experience of the knower). Yet this does not detract from the fact that reality exists, irrespective and outside of our experience. Hence we ourselves prefer to use the term radical relativism in order to emphasize the fact that reality is relative to our perceptions, meaning that it does not reveal itself in an absolute manner, but 'in relation' to perceptions. See Tomàs Ibañez, *Il Libero Pensiero. Elogio del Relativismo*, Milan: Elèuthera, 2007.

up the benefits and the drawbacks. To recognize the positive value of our limits is an essential part of human life experience (as far as body and language are concerned), despite the anxiety may cause us to discover our finitude in both time and space by becoming aware that we are endowed with limited mental and physical resources, in the same way as our the horizon of our planet is limited. Personal autonomy is a process, not a state of nature or something permanent. The interaction between human individuals (and even non-humans) with the products of digital technology and the objects of our everyday world, are not immutably determined and cannot be reduced to axioms from which rules of conduct could be perfectly derived.

There is no need to be an anti-capitalist anarchist in order to understand that libertarianism is grounded on a remarkably impoverished and warped definition of the concept of freedom in order to justify greed. [10] Without going into a detailed refutation of libertarianism, for our purposes here it will suffice to examine the misunderstanding of freedom which is the conceptual basis of anarcho-capitalism. The sphere of freedom is far more complex than the mere freedom of the capitalist market. A positive definition of freedom, meaning one that adds rather than subtracts, and which still has a revolutionary quality, can be found in Bakunin: 'I am truly free only when all human beings, men and women, are equally free. The freedom of other men, far from negating or limiting my freedom, is, on the contrary, its necessary premise and confirmation. It is the slavery of other men that sets up a barrier to my freedom [...] My personal freedom, confirmed by the liberty of all, extends to infinity.' [11]

An individual is not born free by nature, but becomes free through multiple collective processes of liberation. If we want to contrast the two approaches as slogans, we could say that anarchic freedom begins with the freedom of others, whereas from the liberal perspective, freedom needs to be separately constructed for each and every individual. Therefore, for libertarians freedom ends where the freedom of others begins. Nothing could be more remote from the anarchist conception of liberty, which is relative and subject to constant verification, than the purely economic freedom expounded by anarcho-capitalists.

Libertarianism, initially an economic theory eventually became a political philosophy influential among parties, something totally incompatible with anarchism, and even with anarcho-capitalism in the strict sense. Despite this some of its adepts have gone on to defending it in parliament. In the United States there is a libertarian party competing for seats in Congress whose candidate came fourth in the 2008 presidential elections. [12] The US Libertarian Party draws significant support and funding from prominent business people, university professors and politicians. Magazines and think tanks openly claim libertarian leanings and thereby consider themselves to be the most radical and authentic representatives of the true American tradition. [13] In a sense,

---

10   See George Monbiot, 'This Bastardised Libertarianism Makes 'Freedom' an Instrument of Oppression', *The Guardian*, 19 December 2011.

11   Mikhail Bakunin, 'Man, Society, and Freedom', *Bakunin on Anarchy*, trans. Sam Dolgoff, London: Vintage Books, 1971.

12   The US Libertarian has the slogan: 'Minimum government, maximum freedom.' Their website: http://www.lp.org/, features a test where individuals can measure their 'libertarian score'.

13   The Cato Institute, founded in Washington DC in 1977, is the main libertarian think tank in the US, (see: http://www.cato.org). The Ludwig von Mises Institute is more oriented towards economic studies (see: http://mises.org).

the libertarian worldview is reminiscent of the myth of the white frontier man, alone in a hostile environment – but fortunately armed with a gun – setting off to conquer the Far West. Libertarian parties and institutions share a minarchic orientation, they favor a minimal government that has a sole purpose of protecting existing rights. Any interference would lead to an attempt at changing or abolishing the state. This ideology is very close to the Tea Party line.

There are openly libertarian parties in Argentina, Canada and Costa Rica. In Europe Libertarianism is far less common, at least in terms of official policy. Minor libertarian parties can be found in the United Kingdom, Netherlands and there is a libertarian movement in Italy. Though the political agenda of many rightwing parties contains distinctly libertarian elements outside of the United States, Canada and the UK, there is no coherent definition of what it even means to be a libertarian.

In Europe, political movements are developing which are intimately linked with the basic values of libertarianism and they experience a remarkable degree of success, especially among the younger generations. For example 'pirate parties' are becoming increasingly popular. The most important ones are the Piratpartiet in Sweden, the Piratenpartei in Germany, and the Pirate Party in the UK. But there are also smaller pirate parties throughout Europe – in France, Italy, Spain, Austria and the Netherlands. The ideology of the pirate parties appears to becoming global. These parties advocate the abolition of 'intellectual property' and are opposed to the dominant position of corporations and multinational institutions, especially in the digital realm. They also fight increased police powers and surveillance through new technologies. Yet, they would like to realize individual freedom in an ideal technology-driven free market: the internet. There is a debate raging these days about how to define the ideology of these pirate parties, but we should note that none of these parties have a socialist orientation. [14] We will return later on to the links between pirate parties and libertarianism, in the section discussing WikiLeaks.

## 2.03 — TECHNOLOGICAL DARWINISM FROM THE PAYPAL MAFIA TO FACEBOOK: THE IRRESISTIBLE RISE OF ANARCHO-CAPITALISM

Following this outline of the economic and political framework to our critique, we return now to social networks, and specifically to Facebook. It is no secret that Facebook belongs to the libertarian realm in the US – it even has associations with the extreme fringe of anarcho-capitalism. European news covered this issue several years ago. [15] At first glance, this story holds appears to have little relevance to the growth of Facebook, but in fact it is of crucial importance, because it shows that the world's largest social network is actually part of a more extensive strategy to propagate the values and practices of libertarianism.

In the first part of this book, we have used Facebook as an example of a social network whose modus operandi is alien to the way we experience things. This does not mean that the other major social media companies (Twitter, LinkedIn, Google+ etc.) are immune to criticism. What is true for Facebook is also true for the others, companies despite the vast differences in their targeted

---

14    For a good overview on this issue see: https://cabalamat.wordpress.com/2010/02/16/the-pirate-party-is-more-libertarian-than-the-libertarian-party/.

15    See in particular: Tom Hodgkinson, 'With Friends Like These...', *The Guardian*, 14 January 2008, http://www.theguardian.com/technology/2008/jan/14/facebook.

audience and social impact. For the sake of our analysis we will focus attention on the entrepreneur Peter Thiel, a stereotypical anarcho-capitalist. Note that not all social media platforms are as closely linked to anarcho-capitalism as Facebook is. But just as Facebook typifies commercial platforms sociality, Thiel is representative of the spirit of libertarianism within informs ventures capital financing in Silicon Valley. Through our analysis of Thiel we can consider the mentality of Silicon Valley venture capitalists and how they impact on contemporary society.

Peter Thiel was the first outside investor in Facebook, with an angel investment of 500,000 US dollars in 2004, thus holding 3% of Facebook's shares. He planned to cash out his holdings when the lockup expired, no matter what price Facebook's shares were trading at. In August 2012 he has sold off most of his stake, turning his initial investment into more than 1 billion dollar in cash. Thiel made his name as a celebrated venture capitalist in the San Francisco Bay Area managing among others, the Clarium Capital hedge fund (with a 3 billion dollar portfolio) and the Founders Fund. Born in Frankfurt at the end of the sixties, he studied at Stanford, the cradle of Californian hyper-capitalism. At 47, Peter Thiel is amongst the 400 richest men on the planet. [16] He contributed generously to ultra-right, libertarian Congressman Ron Paul's presidential campaign fund when he stood up against George Bush in the republican primaries. He is also member of the Bilderberg Group, an annual private conference gathering together politicians leaders and experts from finance, industry, academia and the military officials, industrialists and bankers to discuss international problems. He has also forcefully expresses his political opinions on Cato Unbound. [17]

One of Tiel's pet projects is the radical critique of the social and political system of the United States and by extension the entire system of Western values, this is because the United States pose as the standard bearers of freedom worldwide. Democracy, according to Thiel, cannot be reconciled with freedom, because nation-states and other so-called democratic institutions stifle individual liberties. On this particular point, we actually could agree, as libertarians, in the traditional, socialist meaning of the word. Representative democracy in its current form is far removed from the idea of direct democracy, or of the free and autonomous management of the commonwealth. Corporate interests, together with the structural crossovers between organized crime, institutions, and major financial and economic groups have all too often reduced democracy to an absurd ritual on election day. Yet Thiel's approach in other respects is openly reactionary and misogynistic.

'Since 1920, the vast increase in welfare beneficiaries and the extension of the franchise to women — two constituencies that are notoriously tough for libertarians — have rendered the notion of 'capitalist democracy' into an oxymoron'. [18] Peter Thiel is a proponent of extreme capitalism without any restraints. [19] His position is beyond that of a mere critic of socialism; he is quite simply anti-social. Along with numerous other influential figures, Thiel is a staunchly advocate of technological Darwinism, a new version of social Darwinism, this time framed in terms of tran-

---

16    See, http://www.forbes.com/profile/peter-thiel.

17    See, http://www.cato-unbound.org/.

18    Peter Thiel, 'The Education of a Libertarian', Cato Unbound, 13 April 2009, http://www.cato-unbound.org/2009/04/13/peter-thiel/education-libertarian.

19    See in particular: Peter Thiel, 'The Optimistic Thought Experiment' Policy Review, 29 January 2008. http://www.hoover.org/research/optimistic-thought-experiment.

shumanist eugenics and technology. According to this 'vision', the best technology shall free the most deserving individuals, in order to outgrow the limitations of the human species. The ultimate objective is a superhuman technology, to become an Übermensch free from death.

The concept of well-defined and static identities, which is one of Zuckerberg's mantras, recurs in Thiel's biography where he is openly gay and a strong defender of right-wing gays, to who he make large donations through the American Foundation for Equal Rights and GOProud. He also maintains close relationships with selected politicians, such as Meg Whitman, who he also financially supports. Whitman, an exponent of female emancipationism, is a former CEO of E-Bay (bought by PayPal), and a former republican candidate for the California government in 2010. Thiel, of course, made his fortune cofounding PayPal, currently the most widely used electronic payment system in the world. The political idea behind PayPal was to remove the central banks control of the money supply. This would sound like a brilliant attempt to set the world free, if it did not result in power being centralized in what Peter Thiel himself has proudly dubbed 'The PayPal Mafia', with himself cast in the role of godfather.[20]

In the group of sharks that started the PayPal Mafia, clever financiers, programmers, entrepreneurs, one figure stands out: Max Levchin, the inventor of it all. Mafia is indeed the correct term to use when talking about him, given his contempt for the 'laughable' rules of the liberal market (in fact these rules are ridiculous since they regulate nothing). These regulations have been set by oppressive institutions in order to restrict the freedom of individuals. The term is equally pertinent to the describe the firm's recruitment practices. Google wants the best math graduates, those who dropped out because they were too shrewd and smart. People who are mad workaholics, free of moral dilemmas and ideally they already know each other to create a tight-knit team. Finally but not least the absolute opacity of financial operations at PayPal cannot is typical of a mafia type of operation.

Let us briefly consider PayPal's basic way of operating. If I want to make an online purchase, PayPal is the simplest and most universally accepted method. Since it was founded in December 1998, PayPal promoted itself as the global intermediary for financial transactions between various credit card systems or in the language of Thiel and Levchin, the dream of a private currency without borders. I need only to open a PayPal account, deposit some money, from a credit card or bank account, and at this point I proceed with the purchase. PayPal takes a percentage of each transaction. The seller has to pay an additional fees to get cash in hand, and since PayPal has in fact taken a dominant position in digital payment systems, the money deposited on active accounts is largely virtual. In this sense PayPal's way of dealing with money is just like the banking industry.

Only PayPal is no bank, at least not in the United States where it is operates as an intermediary. In Europe, initially PayPal's registered office was in London, but it only became a proper bank only in 2007 after relocating its headquarters to Luxemburg for tax purposes. It has become impossible for users to get the services a bank is required to provide according to European regulations. Basically no country in the world PayPal forced the company to follow the normal banking rules and this is hardly a non-profit company. Customer service is nonexistent and scams are not uncommon. PayPal is known to regularly blocking users' accounts for various reasons

20    Jeffrey M. O'Brien, 'The PayPal Mafia', *Fortune*, 13 November 2007, http://fortune.com/2007/11/13/ PayPal-mafia/.

(homonyms, suspected fraud, or a mere glitch). The website Cryptome is worth consulting for extensive evidence of how PayPal treats users. Cryptome has been online since 1996, and collates a large number of downloadable documents, censored by governments and corporation around the world. In 2010 Cryptome's PayPal account was suddenly suspended and its funds blocked. [21]

The very controversial sale of PayPal to eBay made Thiel and his associates very wealthy. This was followed by a long series of incredibly lucrative investments, even by the standards of Silicon Valley. LinkedIn, Groupon, YouTube, Facebook, Zynga, Digg, all these 'Web 2.0' firms got funding from members of the 'PayPal Mafia'. This is all documented in the public domain, interested people can be find the details on financial sites such as crunchbase.com – even Wikipedia articles provide links to trustworthy sources.

As for Thiel, he has connections with most of these companies, either because he was one of the founders, or because he sits on the board of directors. These companies all propagate a utopian or messianic narrative of technology. We have enumerated here only a few of the most significant companies. Palantir Technologies Inc., founded in 2004, and co-financed by the CIA, develops tools for analyzing social networks traffic, and has branched into information warfare. [22] Geni, West Hollywood, in business since 2006) is a social network devoted to the reconstruction of family genealogies. [23] The overarching aim is to build a family tree of the entire world population. Registering on the site allows user to upload documents, pictures and videos, and to research the family history of its millions of users and of their ancestors. Halcyon Molecular, Redwood City, has the objective of 'transforming biology into informatics'. It is notable for developing techniques to accelerating the process and reducing the costs of DNA sequencing. [24]

Thiel is funding, or has funded, projects that demonstrate his political aims and reveal his network of support at the same time. Two projects are notable in this regard. The Seasteading Institute of Patri Friedman, the grand-son of ultra-liberal economist Milton Friedman, and son of the anarcho-capitalist economist David Friedman, was founded in order to establish small, autonomous communities on artificial islands. [25] These artificial islands would be located in international seas and therefore beyond any kind of state control. [26] The Singularity University (formerly the 'Singularity Institute for Artificial Intelligence'), aims at researching solutions to transcend the limits of the human body in particular death, by accelerating the 'natural' evolution of a new dominant species, which will arise after the Singularity. [27] Each of these initiatives deserves a separate study. The Singularity Theory espoused by futurologist Ray Kurzweil is widely supported by the Californian transhumanist movement and also by scientists like Marvin Minsky, one of the proponents of

---

21  Andrew Orlowski,'Cryptome: PayPal a "Liar, Cheat and a Thug"', *The Register,* 10 March 2010, http://www.theregister.co.uk/2010/03/10/cryptome_PayPal/.

22  See, https://www.palantir.com/.

23  See, http://www.geni.com.

24  See, http://halcyonmolecular.com.

25  It is curious that Milton Friedman (1914-2006), winner of the 1976 Nobel Prize in Economics, a notable proponent of *Laissez-faire* economics and financial advisor to the Chilean dictator, Augusto Pinochet, has been vigorously attacked by Rothbard, who considered him a statist for his position on government control of the gold reserves and currency issue.

26  See, http://seasteading.org/.

27  See http://singularityu.org and Bruce Benderson, *Transhumain,* Paris: Payot & Rivages, 2011.

strong AI. The discussion on transhumanism may seem fanciful to anyone outside of the cliques of Californian technophiles – but it is equally remote from the concerns of the great majority of human beings whose daily problems are survival, drinkable water, sufficient and not the prospects of technological immortality. Although the enthusiasm for posthuman dystopias is rather limited in Europe, not many voices are raised against the prevailing technophilia. Few question their own dependence on all kinds of technologies from their car to their smartphone. In this sense, it is significant to note that the myth of unlimited growth based on increasing technical efficiency is not actively opposed in the mainstream political discourse of Europe or elsewhere.

In summary, Facebook is part of a game manipulated by the most powerful anarcho-capitalist businessperson in the world. Radical transparency is one of the components of a wider political project that aims at controlling human relations through surveillance technologies. An information war is at hand, autarchic communities of technological elites are being designed outside of national borders while institutes research the possibility of technological immortality. These facts have been known for a long time. Yet the media, web users, activists and people who should possess enough common sense to be concerned about their independence and autonomy, remain silent.

Most of Thiel's political positions remain fascinating, radical, and disturbing at the same time. The emerging ideology is one of frantic, unbridled individualism fueled by a capitalism that is both technocratic and messianic. In open criticism against the curriculum of elite American universities, Thiel launched a support program in September 2010 for aspiring young people under twenty who are willing to start their own company without following a traditional university education. The 20 under 20 Thiel fellowship program has funded twenty 'young promising individuals', who will each receive a hundred thousand US Dollars over a two year period. Free enterprise and meritocracy are the vital terms here. Seen through Thiel's eyes it is not the internet which created a bubble of vacuous behavior; it is the American education system which is no longer able to exploit true innovation. Therefore only total privatization will be able to open the doors of a prosperous technological future.[28]

In a more theoretical text, very tellingly titled 'The End of the Future', Thiel depicts the current stagnation we are living in and points out the fact that there is little investment in cutting edge technology with few investors being prepared to back high risk future projects.[29] According to Thiel this the root cause of today's social, cultural, and economic crisis. The United States, traditional defenders of innovation and ' the next big thing', have fallen into a prolonged period of inertia. As the US is the economic leader of the West, Thiel assumes the rest of the world will be following suit. Thiel sees the crisis of the West in terms of the vanishing frontier, that needs to be endlessly pursued, the frontier that is an essential trope of the American Dream.

He often public expressing his profound disappointment at the fact that Silicon Valley entrepreneurs are dedicated exclusively to profit and have little interest in pressing global problems. For Thiel, capitalism is a truly revolutionary tool that, thanks to technology will liberate the human

28  Sarah Lacy, 'Peter Thiel: We're in a Bubble and It's Not the Internet. It's Higher Education', *Techcrunch,* 10 April 2010, http://techcrunch.com/2011/04/10/peter-thiel-were-in-a-bubble-and-its-not-the-internet-its-higher-education/.

29  Peter Thiel, 'End of the Future', *National Review,* 3 October 2011, http://www.nationalreview.com/article/278758/end-future-peter-thiel.

species. But if capitalism has already triumphed, what then remains to be saved? Simple, we have to make capitalism better and the mantra of this current phase is 'green capitalism' and clean technology. Sure, we know that 'green capitalism' is a hoax which has the sole purpose of maintaining current consumption and pollution levels while pursuing increasingly unsustainable growth. But official environmentalism, which has very little to do with a real protection of the environment, is probably preferable to open contempt towards the ecosystem. When it comes to predatory capitalism, the former godfather of the PayPal Mafia has clear ideas: the anarcho-capitalist revolution requires faithful, excited consumers on the one hand, and priests, bishops, and popes with deep pockets on the other. The merchandise must move between the two quickly and always be in stock. Limits to the availability of natural resources cannot be tolerated in a free market where everyone wins. In this case shifting to cyberspace might be a better option rather than attempting to manage all the material problems arising from a frenzied development in the real world. Therefore in addition to quantity and speed, we can add a third vital term: 'waste'.

Thiel is a fierce opponent of any attempt project designed to improve energy efficiency. According to Thiel, no serious venture capitalist should invest in projects that involve 'clean' technologies – a euphemism that has replaced 'appropriate' and 'sustainable' in the official discourse. [30] In his turbo-capitalist vision, waste means the refusal of limits. Waste is also connected to the need for clearly defined identities and the horror of physical contact and corporeality. This represents the exact opposite of a conscientious, autonomous, and self-managed use of technology to meet individuals and collectives needs and desires. The disposable attitude as a source of physical and psychological waste is not only a consequence of 'abundance capitalism'; it is also a structural requirement of the paradigm of unlimited growth and endless economic expansion of the anarcho-capitalist individual's liberty to act. In this atmosphere of megalomania and unfettered expansionism characteristic of big tech firms, waste also returns in the constant change in function and new app developments. Enormous waste fits into the long-term process of distancing and rejection of the physical body, which we discussed in the first part of the book. We will discuss this in greater detail later on.

In conclusion, it is quite easy to analyze the way Facebook operates yet nonetheless one sees a number of culture-related issues appear in the background. To keep track of all the activities of Peter Thiel is an almost impossible undertaking. The message he conveys through the work of his foundation can be just as confused as is any of the ideas espoused by anarcho-capitalists. We read that the Thiel foundation 'defends and promotes freedom in all its dimensions: political, personal, and economic'. [31] Projects supported by the foundation are asked about frontier technologies, non-violence and freedom. Among them, Imitatio.org (inspired by René Girard's Mimetic theory) explicitly presents tech company founders as new society leaders, promoters of freedom that are almost gods, as Thiel himself explained in his article 'Gods, Victims & Startups'. This begs the question, what kind of freedom is this? What type of society are anarcho-capitalists creating with their funds?

---

30   Eric Wesoff, 'Peter Thiel Doesn't Like Cleantech VC, Mankind', *Green Tech Media*, 14 September 2011, http://www.greentechmedia.com/articles/read/peter-thiel-doesnt-like-cleantech-mankind.
31   Geert Lovink, *The Principle of Notworking: Concepts in Critical Internet Culture*, Amsterdam: Amsterdam University Press, 2005, http://networkcultures.org/blog/publication/the-principle-of-notworking-geert-lovink/.

## 2.04 — SOCIAL NETWORKS THROUGH THE ANARCHO-CAPITALIST LENS – OR THE MANAGEMENT OF SOCIALITY IN THE ERA OF BIG DATA

Social networks predate the internet. Sentient beings in general and in particular human beings, need to develop relationships among each other. Few things indeed are worse than loneliness. Even violent criminals, hardened by the prisons' inhuman conditions of detention, shudder at the prospect of solitary confinement. May testimonies of prisoners of war reveal that would rather face physical torture than solitary confinement, since at least there is contact with their torturer. Several scientific experiments conducted on sensory deprivation have demonstrated that a healthy individual, if immersed in a liquid at body temperature and deprived of auditory and visual stimulation, rapidly looses any awareness of the boundaries of his own body and risks insanity, obsessed with the sound of his own heart. It is only through the acceptance of one's own limitation that overcoming solitude in a way that is not harmful to others becomes possible. Rising above loneliness through socialization means that we recognize our own limitations and open ourselves to creative sharing. According to Luce Irigaray: 'The proximity of the other, or more precisely with the other, is discovered in the possibility of creating a common world with him or her which does not destroy the personal world of either one. This common world is always in the act of becoming.' [32]

The need to contact within our own species is not limited to mere survival activities (obtaining food, protection against predators, reproduction), and this need grows with the increase in neuronal complexity. [33] Among humans (but equally among great apes) the relational dimension slowly begins to break away from the individual, literally thanks to the technè, which impacts on our relationships and is the connection between the self, peers, and the world. The first social mediation tool, in a certain sense the first social medium, was probably fire. Instead of huddling together like most social animals do, human groups started to relate to the social medium – fire – by defining a social space organized around that specific technical phenomena. All techniques that evolve into technologies are instruments of mediation in the relationship with the world and with others. Language is the simplest and most powerful instance of this phenomenon: it establishes a separation between the individual and the others (mediation) and permits the projection of past memories (project, desires) into the future. In other words, languages allow us to share personal imagination in a shared, collective imaginary.

The story and the stratification of this complex network of relationships that we call society is a kind of consensual hallucination which we can access through language and symbols by using evolved higher cognitive functions of the neocortex. Animals possessing only a small frontal cortex are less complex than human and are capable of producing practically no artifacts. Neuroscience research demonstrates that when the functionalities of a person's frontal cortex are compromised, she loses the specifically human characteristic of empathy. Such a person will no longer be able to imagine what an other person's experiences may be. Once their reflexive capacity is either damaged or even destroyed, they can no longer perceive themselves as individuals belonging to various social groups such as family, sports teams, groups of friends, social class,

32   Luce Irigaray, *Sharing the World*, London: Continuum, 2008, p. 47.
33   See the work of Boris Cyrulnik in particular: *Ensorcellement du monde* Paris: Odile Jacob, 1997, *Les nourritures affective,* Paris: Odile Jacob, 2000, and *De chair et d'âme,* Paris: Odile Jacob, 2006.

workplace team, local community etc. The meaning usually assigned to things and to the world becomes confused, fluid, ambiguous and ill defined. Nothing makes sense any longer, in a distinct, articulated and communicable way.

To understand the world of which we are part means to position ourselves in an environment which transcends our finitude as individuals in space and time, while still comprehending this environment through a fictional collective idea. The very prospect of imagining and planning a future based on past experience, and then to understand what surrounds us, falters at the moment that we are no longer able to go through and modify in a significant way the networks to which we belong. Even to imagine this has become impossible. Paradoxically, when we are confronted with too many data, we become unable to make sense of any of it. The sheer mass of data and the speed at which information hits us makes any analysis cumbersome, or extends the time required to a potential infinity. Such an analysis hence becomes pointless using the traditional methods. Yet there are two related concepts that allow is to continue exploration and analysis: Big Data and profiling.

At the beginning of the 21st century, one gigabyte (one billion bits, i.e. one billion text characters) seemed like a large amount of data. A decade later, the internet contains a hardly imaginable amount of data, something near five trillion gigabytes, the numbers are predicted to double each year. [34] We will provide two examples in order to grasp this order of magnitude. A high-definition feature film requires several GBs. Currently a personal computer contains more data than an entire family would have been able to produce over several generations. There are billions of site-pages on the internet, but there exists also a large number of unconnected networks which may be larger than anything we can imagine, or even what a human brain can picture. [35] We have entered the era of Big Data and we are still only at the beginning.

In everyday life also, even when if we are not directly involved in the use of the devices generating this data, we are witness to countless occasions for the detection, storage and analysis of data involving almost every human activity. The details are increasing and the resolution is ever more finely honed. Everyday, an extraordinary volume of SMS, emails, calls, posts, images, videos, chats and documents of all types are being produced. There is no way we could be aware of even a fraction of all the data being sent and exchanged via WiFi networks and mobile devices capable of tracing our movement. Search engines register all our requests through logs, cookies

---

34  The figures are taken from the report of the independent analyst firm IDC and should be treat with the usual caution since they are a large multinational company, with their own vested interests. But since the purpose here is purely demonstrative, the precise numbers do no alter our argument. For more information see the 2011 IDC Digital Universe Study http://www.emc.com/collateral/about/news/idc-emc-digital-universe-2011-infographic.pdf and David Bollier, *The Promise and Peril of Big Data*, Washington: The Aspen Institute, 2011, http://www.aspeninstitute.org/sites/default/files/content/docs/pubs/The_Promise_and_Peril_of_Big_Data.pdf.

35  Contrary to what one might imagine, the public knowledge is only a fraction of existing knowledge. Much of the knowledge is secret, state secret or trade secrets, removed from the public eye and largely meant to subjugate and manipulate us. See the comprehensive research undertaken on 'secret materials' by Peter Galison, physics professor at Harvard, especially 'Removing Knowledge', *Critical Inquiry*, 31 (2004) Chicago: University of Chicago Press, https://www.fas.harvard.edu/~hsdept/bios/docs/Removing%20Knowledge.pdf and his documentary film with Robb Moss, *Secrecy*, http://www.secrecyfilm.com/about.html.

and LSOs (local shared objects). Automatic payment systems in toll booths, supermarkets, ATMs record all our purchases. Social networking platforms record all our connections with friends, colleagues, co-workers and lovers. Record, archive and analyze everything at optimal speed. Quantity and speed are always viewed as advantageous.

However, the focus is not on the magnitude of this, inordinate as it may be, but the interrelationship between data and the increasing opportunities to increase access and work from a smartphone, a tablet or computer. Because this data is linked to us, we cannot be dissociated from it and it constitute our digital footprint. Our identity is therefore perpetually reconstructed through data collection and analysis. But this has nothing to do with knowledge: all Big Data can do is to provide ever more opportunities to make profits through profiling.

In the first part of work we have already discussed the construction of a profile, a unique digital fingerprint that identifies individuals as precisely as possible. It is no coincidence that the vocabulary used is 'fingerprint' and 'traces', as if we were on the scene of a crime. Profiling is an activity that originates from criminology. Whenever we use digital tool and services we leave trace that might be subject to profiling through analysis and archiving. The metadata is used from profits, which in turn allows the existence of a 'free' 'Web 2.0'.

Unlike machines, human beings are not able to manage Big Data. Machines can analyze and calculate in an individual's most likely behavior. Recall that for anarcho-capitalists, the individual realizes herself in action, through two variants production and consumption. Since individuals are no longer able to orient themselves in the noise of data that surrounds them, it becomes necessary to delegate tasks to machines. In order to get closer to the ideal society, individuals need to become machine-readable. They must also continuously feed the databanks within ever accelerating feedback loops. Users explicit and implicit preferences are then archived, disaggregated and re-aggregated in real time.

Profiling is the promise of freedom automated: contextualized advertising, research into users' sentiments to provide personalized, tailored ads in order to maximize click-through sales. This is shortly followed by the disposal of the purchase as soon as possible in order to purchase a new commodity. We, the users, are all suspects whose most intimate details must be known so we can satisfy our compulsive craving for new and immediately obsolete objects. The problem of privacy is endless discussed, but only enters the public discussion once it has already been violated. This issue is usually coupled with complaints about the immorality of an authoritarian system that divides people into categories. In the era of Big Data conspiracies are rife. But the real problem is much more concrete and distressing because it affects us all personally and not as an anonymous mass. While certain individuals want to be profiled, for the others whatever we do in order to avoid profiling, our digital footprint is inescapable. There is no way we can opt out once enlisted in the army of the data-suppliers. We are all prosumers in the sense that we are both at once the producers and consumers of data.

The problem relating to the use and abuse of data mining have been subject to debate for some time. [36] New lines of digital segregation are being created, based on access, i.e. which research-

---

36   Dino Pedreschi et al, 'Big Data Mining, Fairness and Privacy: A Vision Statement Towards an
      Interdisciplinary Roadmap of Research', *KD Nuggets,* October 2011, http://www.kdnuggets.
      com/2011/10/big-data-mining-fairness-privacy.html.

ers, institutions and groups have the means and the opportunity to use this data? What are the rules, what are the limits and who decides? Here is not the place for a detailed examination. [37] We will return to our main point here. This is not about going against progress and its promise of a brilliant future, nor is it an escape into Luddism or into its exact opposite, cryptography. To hide serves no purpose; neither does refusing to come to terms with the present order of things. What we need to do is to get a clear understanding of Big Data and profiling, in so far as practical strategies for the realization of a society modeled on anarcho-capitalism, an ideology according to which everyone is 'free' to rob everybody else. The anarcho-capitalist 'utopia' can more accurately be termed a dystopia, based on control and self-control. We are imperceptibly drifting from a world rich with meaning from relationships to one that where meaning exists only through connections relayed by machines.

It seems we no longer need either theories or practices that are grounded in personal belief and proved by life experience. The status of knowledge is transformed, because it seems that the figures speak for themselves. Knowledge emerges from data as self-evident and imposes itself as a certainty. Statistical correlations establish relationships between things and have a bear on relationships between people. We no longer shape a discourse; data is to have the last word. This is the chimera of a data-driven society, where the role of the human subject is practically irrelevant. The role of humans now is one of docile acquiescence where we relinquish out ability to choose and desire. It seems a parody of the ancient Delphic maxim 'know thyself', and instead is the messianic promise of the Quantified Self movement, 'Self-knowledge through numbers'. Give us ever more powerful machines, handover all your data, be transparent and we can predict the future. The future of the market, of course.

We fly over the world, we consider it from the outside, we see oceans of data, expanding and swirling, transformed by tsunamis of social trends, as sudden as it is fleeting, occupying all available space before giving way to the next start up. We can analyze the attitudes of the masses and the aggregate opinion is easy to obtain through polls and data mining. [38] We, the targets are enthusiastic and willing victims; we love to be 'free' consumers. The general, global recording of everything is the price to be paid if we want to be truly 'free' to choose. An algorithm can inform us of what we truly want: it already advised which book to buy on Amazon. Algorithms correct our Google searches, suggest to us which new film we should see and tells us which music best suits our taste. It is an algorithm that tells us of our potential friends on Google+, LinkedIn, Twitter and Instagram. Algorithms are paying attention for us, and encourage correct socializing. In the near future it will be no longer be necessary to desire anything, since an algorithm will know our desires before we do.

This future will be the equivalent of seeing with 'the eye of God', who is able to predict the future in the crystal ball where the deluge of information flows. Open your heart, let your body be dissected into useful segments, speak your mind, tell us where you are now, what it is you are

---

37   For a good critical overview see, Danah Boyd and Kate Crawford, 'Six Provocations for Big Data', *A Decade in Internet Time: Symposium on the Dynamics of the Internet and Society,* September 2011, http://papers.ssrn.com/sol3/papers.cfm?abstract_id=1926431.

38   The latest software for understanding social network dynamics and social influence is SenticsNet http://sentic.net/.

doing, and who is your current company. Without thinking say it all, now, and you will obtain all you desire, without even knowing yet what it is you actually desire. Inexpressible vertigo (in the literal sense of what 'cannot be'), infantile enthusiasm (in the original sense of *infans*: the one who does not talk yet), mystical ecstasy in front of the Matrix before our very eyes. The expressions and imagery about Big Data often take on a religious tone, and that is a bit too frequent to be mere chance.

A kind of techno-fascistic religiosity is the fetish underlying the knowledge society of Big Data. It is an indifferent religion since having a sufficient quantity of data, means any viable hypothesis can be confirmed. Like the Bible, the Q'uran or any holy book, the scope for interpretation is endless, yet Big Data is vastly larger. It is precisely because Big Data is so vast that is can be manipulated to accommodate and support any assumption. Statistics can be used for everything but ultimately prove nothing, they are apparently scientific proofs of highly ideological presuppositions.

Meanwhile, paraphrasing John Lennon, *life is what happens to us while we're busy* amending our digital profiles and contributing to an even mass of data. One could argue that there are inherent limits to digital computing and that the libertarian faith in innovation without limits is a logical absurdity. But even in the absence of limits, this faith is an irrelevance, as we would not longer be able to manage our data in an autonomous fashion anyway. We would no longer be able to manage the very knowledge that keeps us afloat. So time to put aside the illusions of omnipotence and to descend to Earth. Performing a specific search with a concrete and defined aim exposes the trap lying behind the sheer endless availability of data. Our goal is to write a work for curious people. There is a great difference between writing a serious essay and making an endless compilation, and inevitably imperfect still, of critiques, general observations and alternative proposals. The mere accumulation of more data does not by itself result in a better quality of research. There is not such thing as an objectively superior choice because it supposedly represents the 'natural' outcomes of a search from an unbelievable quantity of data. Worse still, the data is often automatically deemed correct, and neutral, just because it is derived from sensors placed on the body using wearable computing devices. There are only subjective, well-defined choices, when personal preferences are passionate pleas for something that we do not like, just for the duration of a click, but we are willing to become involved because it matters to us.

## 2.05 — THE HACKER SPIRIT AND THE DISEASE OF ANARCHO-CAPITALISM

There are some people who absolutely love machines. They must know how devices work, and nothing will mitigate their curiosity, least of all the fear of being punished for breaking the law. They enjoy taking machines apart and putting them back together, tinkering with them in the process to improve their performance. In the case of digital devices they write codes to make them interconnect and to function in a new way. They literally feed the machines and give them new life. These passionate people are hackers.

There are various types of hackers. Code hackers write in various computing languages – and their 'dialects' – to create new programs. Security hackers invent novel ways of bypassing or breaking a system's protection. Sometimes they actually put this knowledge to work, but often they just make their discoveries public. They sometimes can be found working for large corporations, governments, institutions or the army. In these cases they are supposed to enhance the security of computer systems. Hardware hackers are more interested in directly altering machines: cutting, soldering, assembling and fixing not only computers but also radios, stereos, and even, bicycles, toasters and washing machines. Geeks on the other hand, may not always possess expertise in coding, but they move effortlessly in the digital realm, and can create and modify to audio, video, and text objects, and use communication tools like IRC (Internet Relay Chat).

In the mainstream press, hackers and geeks are often portrayed as repressed and brilliant adolescents who threaten to take down the whole digital world from their obscure rooms filled with computers and modified devices. Totally withdrawn in their own universe, they are more at ease in front of a computer screen than facing a real human being. They are nerds: physically below average, poor at sports, shy with girls and lacking of social skills. But they do possess other abilities, in particular the ability to adeptly use computers. They have a power they can put to use wherever it suits them: they potentially can destroy your data on a whim, or for money or, to take revenge against world that does not seem particularly interested in them.

These simplifications however, do not do justice to the complexity of the hacker phenomenon. This stereotype makes no distinction between the mercenary hackers training the military for cyber warfare, and the 'script kiddies', who use viruses and malware they downloaded from the internet. The mythical figure of the hacker breaking into databases, stealing private information and mocking the police is the most widespread representation of an enduring maxim: knowledge is power. Mastery of technology generally is a source of power. Knowledge-power is a social power in the same way as a tribesman who can handle fire may establish himself as the leader of the tribe, or as a shaman, to whom the leader of the tribe must respect in order to gain from this technical power only he can handle. Whoever has the knowledge can make use of it to become superior to others and exert authority. Knowledge about machines, in a world shaped largely by the machines themselves, is the greatest possible power that exists in our age. The control of this power creates an unrelenting struggle for supremacy.

Nerd supremacy has ancient roots. In a society that is run by machines, it is logical to assume that those who master the machines also command society. Though the specifics may not yet be clearly established, it is at least arguable that a certain type of relationship style has impact on most of the technical instruments we make daily use of and which shape the way we interact with each other. It makes no sense to seek for the absolute truth, nor to figure out what is a 'real' hacker. If we were to analyze thousands of individual cases and personal stories about hacking, we would be left with such diversity that we would not be able to come to a valid interpretation. There is no doubt we could marshal enough 'evidence' if our aim was to prove that hackers are dangerous criminal, but we could equally come up with 'proof' that hackers are actually exemplary citizens, fearlessly fighting against multinationals, banks, and authoritarian governments to create a more free world.

Instead, let us rather observe that among the most influential and powerful individuals in the world of today, whether it is in the 'real' economy or in the realm of the imaginary, we find many hackers, ex-hackers and aspiring hackers. It is uncertain to what extent Bill Gates, Microsoft's founder, and Steve Jobs, founder of Apple, are hackers but is well known that the Silicon Valley of the seventies was the common denominator for them both. Larry Page and Sergey Brin founded Google at Stanford University, and following the classic geek tradition, relocated to a garage in order to house the machines running their nascent search engine. They might be hackers with commercial ambitions, unlike Steve Wozniak – Apple's other Steve, but it can not be denied that they possess IT expertise. As can be seen in the feature film The Social Network, Mark Zuckerberg is very much at ease with machines, so much so that he had devised a computer-assisted dating system, which we now know as Facebook. Julian Assange, the controversial front man of WikiLeaks, has a past as Australian security hacker before he challenged governments across the world by publishing secret diplomatic cables. Linus Torvalds, creator of Linux operating System, is typical of many hackers who devote their time trying to write better code than everybody else. Possibly less well known to the public is Richard Stallman, the founder of the Free Software Federation (FSF).[39] He is perhaps the best example of the purist hacker following his own ideals of freedom without any compromise.

It is very important to understand the values that underlie what has been called 'the hacker spirit' or even 'the hacker ethic'. This because these values profoundly shape the collective, technological imaginary, digital sociality and ultimately the society in which we live as a whole. We must look beyond hagiographic reconstructions of a mythical past where lanky and bespectacled heroes of the digital revolution, with a twisted and odd sense of humor are driven by pure love of knowledge and a peculiar notion of fun.[40] Human actions are never pure, nor can they be predicted by some automated pattern or at least not yet. Simplistic trivialization of the apparent differences between good and bad, 'white hats' versus 'black hats' hackers, or between hackers who have sold out to corporation and governments versus those who remain independent only serve to obscure a proper understanding of the hacker spirit. The irreducible differences of individual stories are, as always, a starting point for observation. But the question remains – do these differences also betray similarities? Is there something like a 'hacker style'?

Ippolita has a strong bias in favor of those individuals who get their hands dirty and attempt to lead an autonomous life. One of the mottos that describe the hacker attitude is 'hands on', put your finger on it. Another motto is 'information wants to be free': we should reject all barriers. To achieve this goal, hackers share what they learn and explain their techniques and strategies, which is also the way of gaining merit in the hacking community. From a political viewpoint, when hackers and geeks talk within their community, the use of the word freedom is frequent, as in freedom of expression, of thought, in private life, as an individual, etc. The other dominant concept is individual meritocracy. In the United States this sentiment more or less corresponds with the liberal world-view. But there are so many subtle shades in the spectrum that the original color tends to fade away.[41] If Zuckerberg and Stallman are total opposites of each other, it may well be that their unexpected similarities are revealed precisely by this opposition. The former spends his time harvesting web users personal contents through proprietary software, you can't download or modify Facebook's code, in order to reap large profits from individually

39  Richard Stallman's Free Software inspired the Open Source movement and was very influential within the digital culture right from the beginning.

40  The best-known hagiography, which is still a good historical reconstruction, is Steven Levy's Hackers, Heroes of the Computer Revolution, New York: Penguin, 1984.

41  Gabriella Coleman is one of the few scholars who try to go beyond the stereotypes. See: Gabriella Coleman, 'Hacker Politics and Publics', Public Culture, New York: Institute of Public Knowledge, 2011, http://gabriellacoleman.org/wp-content/uploads/2012/08/Coleman-hacker-politics-publics.pdf.

targeted adverts. The latter appears to be completely committed to protecting the software's basic freedoms: execute, modify, distribute and share. Nonetheless, both are somehow hackers.

The common character trait both of them share is their individualistic tendencies. There are very good reasons for this: even from a purely technical viewpoint, sharing is only possible among individuals if they are able to create personal projects. Besides, in more prosaic terms, the relationship between a person and her computer had become so closely personal from the 1980s onwards that it borders on solipsistic alienation.

There are other remarkable similarities. The cult of excellence, for instance: permanent improvement is imperative. A third characteristic is the rejection of limits as a principle. Overcoming obstacles, crossing boundaries, penetrating systems, is the language used to describe the rush into technical space, which, with the advent of the internet, had become a true virtual space in itself. The tendency to set challenges, like 'which of us will get furthest' is the outcome of individual excellence coupled to the will to explore the unknown. In its crudest form this takes the shape of a duel between two opponents. But there are more complex configurations, all subsumed under the competition principle which in itself is typically a male behavior. Not surprisingly hackers are overwhelmingly males, with a high level of education, an inclination towards abstract thinking, and often diagnosed with Asperger syndrome. [42] To develop from a small clique of computer geeks to a vast corporate hierarchy, takes less time than one would think. Communities of hacker-geeks celebrate meritocracy, risk-taking, the need for maximum commitment, and finally the duty to think independently before pestering your geek friends with basic questions, a precept epitomized by the acronym R.T.F.M. – *Read The Fucking Manual*. A community consisting of people who are able to understand and appreciate individual effort also knows how to add value and agree on a shared cause of knowledge. The explicit references to personal charm, pride for discovering an elegant solution quicker than anyone else and technical expertise acquired at a high price are all recurrent motifs of hacker culture. [43]

The individual engaging in hacking is surrounded by an aura of sorts, conferring on him a kind of superior power. On the other side are the non-hackers, the users or the sheep who understand nothing about computers. Manuals and guides are published for these users, often called lamers – it is even possible to teach them how to use certain programs! But it remains a common sense fact that knowledge has a pyramidal structure. There are exoteric levels, understandable to the general public, and

---

42   Asperger syndrome is an autism spectrum disorder, and involves socializing difficulties and stress. It has been noted that San Francisco's Bay Area has by percentage many more cases of Asperger's than the US national average. In 2011, lawyers in the United Kingdom used Asperger's as an extenuating condition in order to reduce the sentence of Ryan Cleary, an alleged member of the notorious 'Lulzsec' hacker group. We will go more into the 'Lulz spirit' (Laughing out Loud) later on, it suffices here to say that it consists of breaking into secured systems, extracting private data and publishing it.

43   FAQs (Frequently Asked Questions), a repertoire of questions and answers that show how to use a services, programs and tools, demonstrates in an impressive manner this very belief, that the individual must show that she has done all she can for herself before asking for help. This approach can take various forms, some more community oriented through prioritizing the necessity to develop shared knowledge, but under no circumstances should shared knowledge be seen as some kind of pre-digested pap accessible to all. The ability to find your own way out when challenged by a novel situation, and to apply a creative solution to the problem has obvious parallels to the myth of the explorer, able to orient herself in an unknown territory by reading and interpreting the clues she discovers around her.

esoteric levels only open to the initiated. There are many levels of initiation and competence, referred to in the stereotypical distinction between those who belong to the elite in terms of being familiar with machines and those who are mere amateurs. [44]

From this state of mind arises two behavioral characteristics: one is a thinly veiled contempt of the physical body, the real world and for physical contact with other human beings. The second characteristic is a tendency to see everything in black and white, like a transposition of the ones and zeros in binary code. Either it is right or wrong, good or bad. The world is an epic battle between the forces of good and evil, the dark forces have a global impact. The knights of Knowledge, the Jedis of the machines, may chose for one side or the other, but it is clear there is war and those who have more weapons cannot remain mere spectators. We are drawing a caricature to describe these competing traits but many examples are consistent with this vision. A spirit of confrontation lingers.

Individualism and the cult of limitless liberty are two major traits shared by both the hacker spirit and anarcho-capitalists. We can add to that a blind faith in the redeeming power of technology. We should also note that both anarcho-capitalists and hackers share the same enemy: institutions, and more specifically US federal institutions, which impose limits on their liberties (unrestricted access to knowledge in one case, unrestricted freedom to get rich in the other). Yet if we are to believe Eric S. Raymond's half-serious pronouncements, the points of agreement go much further. Eric Raymond himself is a high-ranking, 'historic' member of the hacker tribe and a dyed-in-the-wool libertarian. In his portrayal of the fictitious person J. Random Hacker, he describes his political convictions as follows:

> Formerly vaguely liberal-moderate, more recently moderate-to-neoconservative (hackers too were affected by the collapse of socialism). There is a strong libertarian contingent which rejects conventional left-right politics entirely. The only safe generalization is that hackers tend to be rather anti-authoritarian; thus, both paleo-conservatism and 'hard' leftism are rare. Hackers are far more likely than most non-hackers to either (a) be aggressively apolitical or (b) entertain peculiar or idiosyncratic political ideas and actually try to live by them day-today. [45]

There are good reasons to take this analysis seriously. Even if, generally speaking, hacking is rather apolitical, politics have begun to dominate in the hacking sphere. More than twenty years have passed since the first large-scale suppressive operations against hackers, with 'Operation Sun Devil' as a climax. In the US numerous youths were trampled down during the 'Hacker Crackdown', and its second act a few years later in Italy with 'Fidobust', aka the 'Italian Crackdown. [46] The suspicious attitude of the authorities has not changed ever since. There has been an increase of repressive laws exces-

---

44  For more detail on what we are discussing here and to get to grips with what motivates a hacker, see *Phrack*, one of the best independent publications on hacking which has been active since the mid-eighties: http://www.phrack.org.

45  See Eric S. Raymond, *The Jargon File*, https://web.archive.org/web/20130827121341/http://cosman246.com/jargon.html Despite being somewhat egocentric and a bit dated by now, *The Jargon File* (archived August 27, 2013) remains a fundamental document to understand the history and culture of hacking up to the beginning of the 21st century.

46  See Bruce Sterling, *The Hacker Crackdown: Law and Disorder on the Electronic Frontier*, New York: Bantam Books, 1992, http://www.mit.edu/hacker/hacker.html and Carlo Gubitosa, *Italian Crackdown: BS amatoriali, volontari telematici, censure e sequestri nell'Italia degli anni '90*, Milan: Apogeo, 1999.

sively widening the scope for surveillance and banning hacking-associated initiatives. Exemplary in this respect are the Digital Millennium Copyright Act (DMCA) in the United States and the European Union's Copyrights Directive (EUCD). Conflicts in the 'real' world have now shifted into the 'virtual' world giving a new lease of life to old antipathies. Keywords like labor, class and property see themselves updated into a Web-compliant jargon. Large numbers of people are being criminalized on the pretense of protecting copyrights, which all too often are a mere scapegoat for corporate greed. Where some see virtual worlds as open playgrounds, for the unscrupulous and acquisitive they are empty lands ripe for conquest.

'The Underground Myth' is an article that puts the acts of hackers into proper historical context and describes the ongoing process where control of the internet is increasingly concentrated in the hands of a few firms and institutions. [47] All these organizations have largely benefited from the contributions of these kids, whom they criminalized out of curiosity only to co-opt them shortly afterwards in order to improve their security systems, i.e. to build improved controllable networks. The 'digital piracy' allegory is therefore very appropriate only not in the sense intended by corporations. The way cyberspace is being occupied has much in common with the way America was conquered. The 'frontier' trope recurs, and with it, that of colonization and the unavoidable violence associated with it. The abuses and massacres perpetrated in order to spread 'civilization', together with material, human, and animal losses incurred were not mere 'collateral damages', but they were essential to the colonizing mission. In the same fashion, the conquest of the digital realms implies pyramids of profiteering abuses at the global scale and enormous pile-up of electronic waste and obsolete code. In order to make all this possible, it is necessary either to buy out or destroy the pirates infiltrating the digital oceans. [48]

In the 17th and up to the early 18th century, pirates in the New World had a more adventurous, and also more free and egalitarian life than the sailors on Spanish, British, French or Dutch ships. [49] Later they were often coerced to sell their liberty and enlist under the flag of the various European powers whose ships they previously plundered. 'Letters of Marque' transformed pirates into privateers, or in others words, into mercenaries. In the same fashion, hackers at the beginning of the 21st century were confronted with joint attacks by institutional colonizers and often opted to co-operate with them. From being free explorers they became proficient mercenaries in the pay of companies and governments who are out to establish a new order of things in the digital realm. [50]

---

47  Anonymous, 'The Underground Myth', *Phrack Magazine,* 18 April 2008, http://phrack.org/issues/65/13.html.

48  See our anaylsis in Ippolita, *Open non è free,* Milan: Eleuthera, 2005.

49  Even today, pirates as heroes of the popular imagination embody a very specific worldview based on liberty and equality. They were libertarians avant la lettre in the sense of socialist internationalism. This thesis is supported with a wealth of historic details in Marcus Rediker's research. See: Marcus Rediker, *Villains of All Nations: Atlantic Pirates in the Golden Age,* London: Verso, 2004.

50  Exemplary in this respect is the 'Tiger Team' case. This was the name of a group of security hackers hired by Telecom Italia and the Italian secret services. The team was involved with fraud in the 2006 election and in selling confidential information to French, Israeli, and American secret services. See details see the investigative documentary of Beppe Cremagnani and Enrico Deaglio, 'Gli Imbroglioni' *Diario,* numero speciale 18 e film, 2007. One of the most disturbing characters in this dark story is Fabio Ghioni, a security expert, essayist and novelist. As an instructor of malicious hackers for several government agencies, he is the promoter of the ENOC program (Evolution and New Order Civilization). Perhaps this is just bait for rich people with money to burn but it may also be yet another transhumanist project, since overcoming the human condition through technology, is a recurring obsession for most anarcho-capitalists and technophiles.

The 'global war' frame of mind satirized in the film, War Games has unfortunately materialized in the realm of digital sociality. News reach us everyday about malevolent hackers engaged on this or that front, against white, black, yellow, or red terrorists, all with vague, unintelligible or absurd demands. They are battling or collaborating with intelligence services with underhand deals and suspicious pasts. The once amusing scenarios of gnostic hackers working with the Illuminati and Voodoo gods of cyberspace, has now become a sinister conceit. Cyber warfare is by now an everyday concept. The internet has become an immense resource, but also a threat to the established order. [51] The sheer quantity of computers and their developing processing power can be used to manage flows of malignant data in order to extract private information, or to carry out attacks, as with the armies of zombie computers remotely controlled by other computers (botnet). For example the computers control by government agencies used to shutdown networks. Viruses are created to attacks enemy targets, or to slow down or disable military research programs. Today's wars like the one in Afghanistan, 'in defense of democracy', are fought at a distance with drones, operated by remote control from bases thousands of kilometers away. The modus operandi is precisely the same as that of videogames, only with all to real deadly effects.

Are hackers a menace in such an apocalyptic scenario? Are they buccaneers or privateers? Are they dangerous subversives combating the established order, or are they the hired hands of strong powers with libertarian tendencies? Let us now take a trip to the far North of Europe, to Sweden, where we will find a number of elements in the farrago of hacking, piracy, and libertarianism: the Pirate Bay site, the Pirat Partiet and WikiLeaks.

## 2.06 — PIRATE PARTIES, OR TECHNOLOGY IN POLITICS

In 2003 digital pirates began infiltrating Sweden's social-democratic society. Since this year the Pirate Bay has been indexing torrent files and saving names and addresses of shared files through the peer-to-peer torrent protocol, a meta-data format that identifies text, audio, and video files. [52] Shared files are not stored on a centralized, server: they are only indexed so as to make them accessible to users. This approach enables Pirate Bay to bypass, the problem of complicity in copyright infringement, which led to Napster's closure in 2001, Morpheus and Grocker in 2003, and numerous other file-sharing systems. According to the reasoning of the Pirate Bay, violations, if they occur, are entirely the users' responsibility. The Swedish pirates regularly publish on their site the legal letters they receive from Microsoft, Apple, Dreamworks and Adobe, as well as the mocking responses they send back to these tech giants.

---

51  'The Threat from the Internet: Cyberwar' *The Economist*, July, 2010, http://www.economist.com/node/16481504.

52  Since 2009 p2p sharing systems have increasingly shifted towards the use of *magnet links*, the traces (*hash*) files rather than names and addresses, substantially reducing the flow of metadata and hence the bandwidth required. The Pirate Bay, like many other similar services started to promote the use of DHT (*Distributed Hash Table*) and PEX (*(Peer Exchange*) as substitutes for traditional centralized *trackers*. Their main benefit is to avoid the need for users (*peers*) to refer to one single server keeping and distributing the names and traces of torrent files. Combined with the use of encryption for incoming and outgoing data flows at the *peer* level, decentralized protocols strengthen the network, making it both safer and more reliable, and, of course, much less prone to interception.

But what, then, is the specific crime that these pirates are accused of? Here, the concept of piracy must be seen in the context of the conflict between big media enterprises operating like a cartel and the practice of sharing copyright protected files. The organizations representing the interests of big firms which produce and distribute multi-media content make use of the 'piracy' moniker to stigmatize the theft of copyrighted content, which lowers their earnings. Their reasoning is that every time someone downloads a copyright protected film (or an audio file, book, video game etc.), that person will not go to the movies, nor will she purchase the product in another legal form. Therefore there is considerable economic damage resulting from this theft.

Let us assume, for the sake of the argument, that private property should be defended when you harm the economic interests of others. The a priori argument in opposition to this is that our purchasing is artificially constrained while there is an enormous proliferation of content in all mediums. In other words, if I have only ten euros to spend on records, there is no way I will be able to spend one hundred. But I can download music for free, usually with a significant compromise in quality as mp3 cannot compete with a high quality vinyl, nor can streaming video be compared with a cinema screen. Many consumers may wish to buy more books, films, or records yet they must limit themselves to what surplus cash they have. In many cases if these contents were not free, they would not 'consume' them. In this sense, there is no real loss in earnings. But there is also an a posteriori argument that can be made with the benefit of hindsight, the increasing turnover of the entertainment industry globally proves that cultural content is a source of profits. Yet greed knows no limit and the idea that profits can grow exponentially is the dream of every boss of a major media company.

There are also legal reasons that make this definition of 'piracy' problematic. Theft of a digital goods that can be identically reproduced at very low cost (memory drive plus the electricity needed to make a copy) is starkly different from the theft of a non-digital good.[53] A copied file does not dispossess the original owner of the file. It follows that intellectual property of this type of goods needs to be distinguished from the property of non-digital goods. Furthermore making file sharing illegal, under any circumstance, tends to erase the difference between commercial and personal use. Yet it is obvious that the re-sale for profit of a copyright-protected digital good and the use of it without any profit-making motives are different things altogether. In fact, it is the architecture of the content distribution system itself that traditionally makes extensive personal use possible. A book, once purchased, can be given away, read aloud, or loaned to a friend. Its sentences can be memorized, repeated, rehearsed, modified, and reproduced for personal use. Quoting an author in another book is generally considered a tribute to the author. In no way can this now all be redefined as theft.[54]

In Europe and in the United States, not to mention the rest of the world, the law is inadequate. Where specific, IT-related law has been enacted it tends to limit and suppress personal usage

---

53   The common distinction between tangible and intangible goods is misleading as well as incorrect, and only serves to strengthen the vulgar mass media interpretation. The files are not immaterial, they are precise sequences of electrical impulses stored on enchanced silicon supports. Moreover, without computers and networks they are inaccessible, and the computers and networks are very obviously material.

54   Nonetheless, this is exactly what happens with proprietary software. The Windows 'shrink-wrap' user license states that you are not the owner of the digital good, but that you are merely allowed to use it, without modifying, copying, or sharing it. The same is true, perhaps to an even worse extent with Apple, since it uses the lock-down software previously distributed under a BSD license.

for the benefit of media oligopolies, which have found governments enthusiastic assistants willing to protect and advance corporate interests by legislative means. But far from being universally accepted, accusations of theft are continually raised. Sites like The Pirate Bay's are true 'repositories of collective actions', to quote the term used by the sociologist and political scientists, Charles Tilly and Sidney Tarrow. [55] The mass use of identical duplication services leads to the emergence of zones of economic counter-power, something that economist John Kenneth Galbraith has dubbed compensatory power, a concept quite close to the Post-Marxist notion of 'counter-power'. [56] These zones of counter-power forms lines of resistance against the prevailing power in the absence of competition, and in particularly with the case of Sweden, against the collusion of the state with anti-market forces. The collusion of governments with oligopolies raises serious problems for citizen-constituencies and is discussed by critics as a kind of 'organized crime' related to a wave of de-democratization. What makes such alliances more troubling is the fact that file-sharing has not demonstrably 'damaged' the creative industries as a whole, but appears to have contributed to world-economic transformations including an increase in creative production and an expansion and globalization of media markets. [57]

In a landmark decision, the operators of the Pirate Bay were condemned in 2009 to a prison term of one year and substantial fines. This judgment has been appealed. Apparently under the pressure of powerful cultural lobbies, the Swedish state went for a repressive approach. However one of the judges had an undisclosed conflict of interests, so the case is still far from clear-cut. After having announced a sale that failed, after a blockade, the Pirate Bay is still indexing millions of files. The members have been arrested and prosecuted, but it continues to inspire fear, the Italian government, for example, decided to block access to the site. The site is theoretically beyond reach of Italians, but indirect access is still possible. Through using a proxy, e.g. Google Translate, or other similar systems, users can circumvent this clumsy attempt at censorship. [58]

A small group of 'netizens' deliberately breaking the law online and therefore demonstrating their disapproval of the concentration of economic power is not a new idea. This is clearly a vital concept, since consumer pressure, for example net boycotts, can produce real change. But it is much more difficult to sustain political theories inspired by online strikes, calls for action, demonstrations, and other networked activities, that are leading to the emergence of a new form popular sovereignty which goes beyond the traditional forms. [59] As we will see later on, online activism is often mere slacktivism, and tends to weaken traditional forms of political commitment. The benefit of this approach is that it redirects the attention from what is less important, the economic aspects, in order to focus attention on the pressing social and political issues.

55  Charles Tilly and Sidney Tarrow, *Contentious Politics*, Boulder: Paradigm Publishers, 2007.

56  John Kenneth Galbraith, *The Anatomy of Power*, Boston: Houghton Mifflin, 1983.

57  Leon Tan, 'The Pirate Bay: Countervailing Power and the Problem of State Organized Crime', *C Theory*, November 2010, http://www.ctheory.net/articles.aspx?id=672.

58  See, http://piratebayitalia.com/.

59  Leaving aside the more militaristic visions of multitude opposed to empire, see: Alexander R Galloway's and Eugene Thacker, *The Exploit: A Theory of Networks*, Minneapolis: University of Minnesota Press, 2007.

It is fair to say that the Pirate Bay affair has had a significant political repercussions. The resurgence of the anti copyright demonstrations caused by government repression played an important role in the rise of the Pirat Partiet in Sweden, the first 'Pirate Party' worldwide. By asserting everybody's right to break intellectual property protection laws it considers outdated and illiberal, the Pirat Partiet has had major successes over the past few years, which culminated in the election of two of its members to the European parliament in 2009. There is no doubt about the fact that the increasing number of copyrights, patents, trademarks and non-disclosure clauses have progressively eroded civil and personal liberties. This has occurred with widespread indifference of the public. The creativity of authors, inventors, and researchers has been debilitated in the process by norms which should protect and encourage it instead of defending big business' interests. Often, the 'total war against terrorism and rogue states' has been used as a convenient excuse to authorize all kinds of suppressive measures, which are intended to control the people for the benefit and protection not only of the cultural industries, but equally of Big Pharma and the biochemical and military industries, in short all actors bend on the privatization of knowledge.

In this regard, the debate around SOPA (Stop Online Piracy Act), a bill proposed to the US Congress in October 2011, gives a good summary of the interests at stake. The full title of the proposed act reads: 'to promote prosperity, creativity, entrepreneurship, and innovation by combating the theft of U.S. property, and for other purposes'. [60] So the copyrights owners, meaning the media and entertainment oligopolies wish to pose as innovative defenders of intellectual property against the thieving pirate. The MPPA (Motion Picture Association of America), the RIIA (Recording Industry Association of America) and other media lobbies are pushing for criminalization, in the narrow sense, for anyone who violates the current status, regardless whether this is for personal or any other usage. Yet, we should remember that copyright infringements are already deemed criminal offenses under the DMCA (Digital Millennium Copyright Act) and EUCD (European Union Copyright Directive). Now not only is it possible to criminally prosecute all who facilitate online tracking of copyrighted material, and that means all search engines including Google, Yahoo, and Bing, but also all browsers, such as Mozilla when they are used to track 'illegal' files. Lined up on the other side are all the network intermediaries, which do not produce and do not hold 'protected' documents, but which are used to access these documents. But the oddity here is that Google, eBay, Yahoo!, Facebook, Twitter, etc., who all ostensibly fight for the users' freedom, are in fact, as we have shown, the new masters of the internet. Moreover, all the codes which these tech giant run their systems on are proprietary, opaque, and protected, yet they claim at the same time to be advocates for transparency and openness. The two concepts foster ambivalent practices – at the individual level at least, they are often mere synonyms for 'totalitarian privatization'. In fact, users have to adopt their proprietary tools and contribute to their world privately. Thus we see a transition from the old media oligopolies to the new digital masters. Positive freedom and autonomy in the tech world seems more and more a distant dream.

Thus, both large scale digital intermediaries and the Pirate Party have the same enemy: the media oligopolies. Even though the Pirate Party is not a hackers party, it can still easily pass as the

---

60   H.R. 3261 (112th): 'Stop Online Piracy Act', October 2011, https://www.govtrack.us/congress/bills/112/hr3261/text.

agent of progressive political demands, especially among the young, who have little access to the paradise of compulsive consumption. In a similar manner, the party also opposes arbitrary police checks. The website of the Pirat Partiet stated:

> We wish to change global legislation to facilitate the emerging information society, which is characterized by diversity and openness. We do this by requiring an increased level of respect for the citizens and their right to privacy, as well as reforms to copyright and patent law. The three core beliefs of the Pirate Party are the need for protection of citizen's rights, the will to free our culture, and the insight that patents and private monopolies are damaging to society. [61]

This program may appear excessively minimal, coming from an opposition party. Yet, at the local elections for the Berlin 'Land' parliament, in September 2011, the German Pirates polled almost 9% of the votes, entering into the local parliament. But to go back to Sweden, it soon became clear that these self-professed pirates do not have very little interest in social policies, and are mostly concerned about their own private interests. In 2010, with a media storm raging, the Pirate Partiet hosted on its servers the WikiLeaks site for free, openly backing the project and challenging the Swedish state to support the 'struggle for liberty' by the charismatic Julian Assange and his associates. [62] And thus we are return to the issues of hackers, conspirators, and the global war against the enemies of the freedom of speech.

## 2.07 — THE WIKILEAKS AFFAIR: A FUTILE CHALLENGE OR SENSIBLE DEFIANCE?

Like the Pirate Bay, the WikiLeaks affair is still unfolding. Since this is a *Spectacle*, in the Situationist sense, a new plot twist is always on the cards. However everything that has been written about WikiLeaks betrays a disturbing lack of critical analysis. There is little beyond the trivial standpoints of the 'Like/ Don't Like' variety. Left-wing groups, especially in Europe, consider WikiLeaks a champion of the oppressed daring to challenge corrupt governments. The logic here is once more borrowed from the battlefield; the enemy of my enemy is my friend. Seen from the perspective of governments, or those taking a patriotic or conservative position, WikiLeaks is viewed as a project threatening international diplomacy. It endangers the lives of soldiers of 'the forces of good' who are engaged in peace keeping operations and the war on terror, as well as discrediting governmental institutions. In our opinion, WikiLeaks, despite involving people in good faith, from the point of view of the *Spectacle* is ultimately part of the libertarian galaxy.

Lets briefly summarize the facts. WikiLeaks was founded in 2006, as a site that publishes classified and secret documents. Until 2010 WikiLeaks used the same interface as Wikipedia and described itself as a place where confidential documents may be posted anonymously. The WikiLeaks site then publicly releases the documents once they have been screened. In the beginning of WikiLeaks, posting documents on the site was neither risk free nor very anonymous, and it was only in a later phase only that the WikiLeaks team setup a relatively secure system. The site

---

61   Pirate Party Declaration of Principles 3.2, http://docs.piratpartiet.se/Principles%203.2.pdf.

62   'Swedish Pirate Party to Host New WikiLeaks Servers', *Piratpartiet Presscenter,* August 2010, http://press.piratpartiet.se/2010/08/17/swedish-pirate-party-to-host-new-WikiLeaks-servers/.

won acclaim from the international press in 2007. By this point Julian Assange had proclaimed himself editor-in-chief. Assange, born 1971, is an Australian hacker, and his technical skills are impressive. His contributions to a range of free software coding projects are highly original. [63] Assange was condemned in Australia for what federal institutions deemed to be crimes but his prison sentence was commuted to a fine. Julian Assange made the front-page of newspapers worldwide in November 2010 when WikiLeaks published secret diplomatic documents exposing the US government.

It is not so much the content of documents published on WikiLeaks that is problematic because it is preferable that news circulates, rather than be censored. But the aims and methods of WikiLeaks which come dangerously close to those of Facebook. The idea is to achieve radical transparency, but now at the level of governments: exposing the evils of corrupt governments, and seeking out the underside of the powerful just as we like to do with our 'friends'. Millions of secret documents are then presented to the general public, generating a phenomenon of mass voyeurism that results in mass indifference. We are confronted with staggering revelations: wars are not intended to export democracy, but instead to control oil, uranium, and access to precious earth resources... More shocking perhaps is that the public has become accustomed to believing outright lies such as 'the war for freedom against the axis of evil'.

Julian Assange is the public face of the white knight hackers, who pose as the guardian priests of a liberating technology, and dissidents who are willing to defy the system even at the cost of their own freedom. There are some contradictions of course, but it is all for our own good. The most obvious contradictions is that this battle for transparency demands a semi-secret, opaque organization, run by a clandestine elite with equally secretive funding, and with a single public leader, a charismatic figurehead able to attract the attention of television cameras and who is prepared to argue with presidents and world leaders, in a media war. There is no mediation possible, no work to be done, no commitment to be shown. There is one only truth to consider, the documents made available to us by WikiLeaks. Yet, as we have shown in the case of Big Data, having a massive storehouse of data at your disposal oppresses rather than liberates people, stirring up a feeling of impotence, and making them think the whole issue is futile. Corruption, violence and news about the shocking behavior of the powerful are hardly surprising for anyone who is not totally oblivious to the world around them.

Moreover, the methods of WikiLeaks appear quite unsuitable to other contexts of information censorship. Attacking the United States while being protected under the constitutional liberties granted by European social democracies like Sweden, with the support of libertarian extremists opposed to any form of government, and large Western newspapers, is far easier than confront-

---

63   Perhaps his most interesting contribution was 'Rubberhose', a hidden encryption program he developed together with other hackers. Rubberhose, which is now outdated, provided a way of denying the existence of the part of a hard-drive where encrypted data was stored. Since decryption is basically only a matter of computing power, at least in theory, hiding the existence of encrypted data itself is a clever strategy that considerably enhances the safeness of data. The technique is known as steganography, meaning concealing the very existence of what you wish to keep secret. It is curious that the technique was specifically devised to safeguard human-right activists operating in autocratic states.

ing, authoritarians states like China, Burma, or North Korea, Cuba, Iran, Syria, or Belarus.[64] The emergence of structure like WikiLeaks is simply inconceivable in modern authoritarian regimes, for the simple reason that these regimes exercise an increasingly effective control on network infrastructures and access to networks. Even if something like WikiLeaks were to occur in these societies, authoritarian governments have many options to manipulate public opinion and rid themselves dissidents without dirtying their hands. The work of Evgeny Morozov describes these methods of manipulation in detail.

In Russia, one of the countries most tolerant of piracy, in a manner that is anti-Western and anti-American in particular, young consultants of the regime influence the opinions of the public with great skill. Russian government propaganda often users the exact same manipulative techniques as American spin doctors: blogging, newspaper articles, entire social networks devoted to pro-regime stances, and to vilifying dissidents – with verbal intimidation often preceding physical aggression. In China we have the 'Fifty Cents Party', a moniker referring to the money allegedly paid for each post supporting the government. Armies of pro-government bloggers busy themselves with tweaking Wikipedia entries, and boosting traffic and pro-regime background noise, drowning out the already feeble opposition voices in the process. Saudi Arab princes regularly hire IT experts to monitor the net for information harmful to the regime, which should be refuted, discredited or obscured. Within the 'international community', states behave exactly like individuals when it comes to their digital profiles: they do their best to identify embarrassing behavior among their peers, while trying to hide their own and glorifying their own achievements without any critical perspective. It is both absurd to suppose that populism and greater transparency can really support democratic debate. Authoritarian and democratic regimes both benefit from transparency; but only when applied to their own citizens. The one who manages their information the best wins.

Let us return to the WikiLeaks affair. The choice to publish the classified documents on the war in Afghanistan on July 25th 2010, in five major newspapers (*The New York Times, The Guardian, Der Spiegel, Le Monde, El Pais*) displays the signs of a confused and contradictory strategy. By publishing the leaks in this sensationalistic way, WikiLeaks are largely following the logic of the tabloid and the Society of the Spectacle. Dispatches were continually released for several months until the end of September 2010, when WikiLeaks' German spokesperson, Daniel Domscheit-Berg, left the organization, or was expelled, due to a personal disagreements with Julian Assange. The latter is now subject to an arrest warrant on for a double charge of sexual assault in Sweden, and which was converted, as per the Schengen agreements, to a European arrest warrant in November 2010.

The allegations of rape do not shed a very favorable light on the already controversial figure of Julian Assange, but it is important to note the entire debacle was part of a media spectacle. By delving a little deeper into the matter, we can understand the issue in its full complexity. According to Swedish law, consensual sex without protection may afterwards be interpreted as sexual assault if one of the parties asks for a test for sexually transmitted diseases (STD) and the other party refuses. Since Julian Assange so far refused to submit to a medical checkup, the accusation has been upheld. But refusing to submit to a blood test is different type of issue altogether

---

64   Geert Lovink and Patrice Riemens, 'Twelve Theses on WikiLeaks,' *Eurozine Magazine,* July 2010, http://www.eurozine.com/articles/2010-12-07-lovinkriemens-en.html.

from sexual assault. [65] On December 7, 2010, Julian Assange turned himself over to the London Police. That same day, under pressure of the US Government, Bank of America, VISA, Master-Card, PayPal and Western Union blocked all money transfers to WikiLeaks and froze its accounts. Julian Assange remained in prison until December 16. Almost one year later, Britain agreed to the extradition request by Sweden, who still want to prosecute Julian Assange for sexual assault. Meanwhile, in the United States, several prominent conservative politicians accused Assange as an enemy of the state that must be apprehended, Sarah Palin wished him dead, and many others asked for a reward to capture Assange dead or alive. Even the more progressive politicians the dominant view was that Assange is a dangerous terrorist.

Perhaps the allegations of sexual assault have been fabricated, but what we know for certain, is that Assange has been widely described as an authoritarian, paranoid and inflexible personality. He has been characterized as a person who cannot stand the hassle of human relationship and is totally committed to his own crusade. So we appear to have another fanatic, and more obsessive, who is representative of nerd supremacy. If you need more convincing, just read his unauthorized autobiography, which came out in November 2011. [66] Having spent all the money of the advance on legal costs, Assange subsequently attempted to terminate the contract with his publishing but was refused.

Another thing worth noticing in the WikiLeaks affair is what Julian Assange had to say in an interview with Forbes Magazine in November 2010. He states that he does not consider himself an enemy of the United States nor of global capitalism in general. On the contrary, WikiLeaks disclosures are meant to improve markets' information, since perfect markets demand completely truthful information. This way, people are free to decide on which product to focus. He went on to declare his faith in libertarianism: 'It's not correct to put me in any one philosophical or economic camp, because I've learned from many. But one is American libertarianism, market libertarianism. So as far as markets are concerned I'm a libertarian, but I have enough expertise in politics and history to understand that a free market ends up as monopoly unless you force them to be free. WikiLeaks is designed to make capitalism more free and ethical.' [67]

Of course, Assange is ultimately a victim in this sad story, since has self-imprisoned himself for several years in the Embassy of Ecuador in London in order to avoid arrest. For some he has become a martyr of free speech Yet, WikiLeaks' war has caused collateral damages, and has at least one other obvious victim: the young American soldier and IT specialist Bradley (now Chelsea) Manning, who was accused of downloading tens of thousands of secret documents and passing them on to WikiLeaks while he was serving as computer intelligence analyst in Iraq. From November 2010, Bradley Manning was first detained for 10 months in particularly

---

65   The story is complicated, due to the fact that the two women filed a complaint together. The full allegations against Julian Assange was published by the Guardian. See: Nick Davies, '10 Days in Sweden: the Full Allegations Against Julian Assange', *The Guardian*, 17 December 2010, http://www.theguardian.com/media/2010/dec/17/julian-assange-sweden.

66   Julian Assange, *The Unauthorised Autobiography*, Edinburgh: Cannongate Books, 2011.

67   Andy Greenberg, 'An Interview With WikiLeaks' Julian Assange', *Forbes Magazine*, 29 November 2010, http://www.forbes.com/sites/andygreenberg/2010/11/29/an-interview-with-WikiLeaks-julian-assange/5.

inhumane military prison in in Quantico, Virginia before being transferred to Fort Lavenworth, Kansas. Activists, lawyers, and notable personalities in arts and culture have staged protests worldwide against the barbarous treatment of the 'spy' Manning, whose culpability is still a matter of a debate. [68] Some people have called Manning a hero, and her name forward for the Nobel Peace Prize in 2012. Manning's sad story shows that blatant confrontation against authorities has harsh repercussions in the digital world just as it would in the real world. Opposing the obscurantism of the powerful in favor of transparency by drawing upon the logic of war and the spectacle is the exact opposite of what should be a tangible struggle for freedom, understood as the expansion of personal and collective autonomy. Disagreements within the WikiLeaks organization and Julian Assange's incarceration led to a split and the foundation of OpenLeaks, a project under development that aims at correcting the organizational imbalances of WikiLeaks. [69] In order 'to foster whistle-blowing and make it safer', OpenLeaks attempts to use shared tools, managed co-operatively by a group having recognized expertise in data gathering. The goal was not to directly host leaks of information but rather to provide technological tools to the holders of the classified information, which gives them the means to act autonomously. In this sense, OpenLeaks avoids an approach that is explicitly opposed to governments, and hence differentiates its position from the rhetoric of libertarianism.

Before the advent of WikiLeaks, sites publishing confidential documents did exist, for example the aforementioned site Cryptome. But the WikiLeaks format had a large impact. After WikiLeaks, a growing number of local leak websites developed in France, Bulgaria, Indonesia and Venezuela. Beyond the simple WikiLeaks clones, different approaches were also tried, such as Wikispooks and Israelileaks. Meanwhile, mainstream medias got busy trying to set up secure communication channels in order to receive anonymous leaked material. Including Al Jazeera, The Wall Street Journal and The New York Times among others. [70] There are also agencies specialized in spying services and companies developing methods of anonymous internal information disclosure. None of them are very much public. Globaleaks.org is the only project set up to study the issue from a technical and philosophical perspective and analyses how these structures could be run on a global scale by hackers, while remaining trustworthy, secure, anonymous and free.

But whichever system is used, the main point is still transparency and exposure, which implies the existence of one single truth, since 'the data speaks for itself'. All this would be unnecessary in a society where everybody used Facebook and followed Mark Zuckerberg's radical transparency doctrine. But would we be more free in such a society? The many critiques of Facebook and its underlying libertarian ideology suggest otherwise. Jaron Lanier, one the inventors of virtual reality and a longtime hacker, has pointed out the risks associated with this

---

68  Bruce Ackerman and Yochai Benkler, 'Private Manning's Humiliation', *The New York Review of Books*, 28 April 2011, http://www.nybooks.com/articles/archives/2011/apr/28/private-mannings-humiliation/.

69  The founder is the former German spokesperson for WikiLeaks, Daniel Domscheit-Berg. See http://leakdirectory.org/index.php/OpenLeaks and Daniel Domscheit-Berg, *Inside WikiLeaks: My Time with Julian Assange at the World's Most Dangerous Website*, New York: Crown, 2011.

70  See the 'Leak Site Directory,' a directory of official and community based sites that actively support whistleblowing and leaks about various topics. http://leakdirectory.org.

drift towards nerd supremacy. [71] Lawrence Lessig, liberal jurist and inventor of the Creative Commons licenses, has reservations about WikiLeaks' defense of total exposure, which he considers as a dangerous perversion of the principle of free speech so dear to Americans. [72] Of course these are interventions that attempt to legitimate the status quo. But the question then becomes, how can hackers fight for freedom with radical interventions, but without sliding down into libertarian rhetoric?

## 2.08 — ANONYMOUS, OR OUT OF THE BOX ACTIVISM

Before making the headlines worldwide, that is, prior to the cablegate documents on Iraq and Afghanistan, WikiLeaks had already published a lot pressing news. Some notable examples being the American secret services' plot to assassinate the Somali prince Hassan Dahir Aweys in 2006, the totally inhuman treatment of Guantanamo inmates by American authorities in 2007, and the rampant corruption of former Kenyan president Daniel Toroitich Arap Moi's close circle in 2008. Also in 2008, as noted by Daniel Domscheit-Berg, members of Anonymous approached WikiLeaks with internal documents of the church of Scientology. These documents were immediately published.

The case of the church of Scientology interests us precisely because it relates to Anonymous, which has become the most talked about hackers-activists group over these past few years. Though the Scientology church is a powerful adversary its activities are far easier to uncover than many clandestine dealings by traditional institutions. The cult had managed to silence quite a number of people who attempted to make information about it public. Threats, intimidation and outright persecution, have been their fate especially in case of former members of the church. Anonymous' Chanology Project started in January 2008 in response to the church's attempt to remove a Tom Cruise interview that revealed the inner workings of Scientology. Before involving WikiLeaks, Anonymous posted on YouTube a video-clip with a 'message to the Church of Scientology'. [73] The two minutes clip's conclusion have become the motto most characteristic of Anonymous: 'Knowledge is Free. We are Anonymous. We are Legion. We do not forgive. We do not forget. Expect us!' Anonymous then launched several rounds of DDoS (Distributed Denial-of-Service) attacks to paralyze the sect's servers by overloading them with requests, a type of attack that requires a certain amount of technical competence. [74] The common thread connecting WikiLeaks and Anonymous is transparency, conceived as the ultimate weapon in the fight against opaque, repressive powers. The

---

71   Jaron Lanier, 'The Hazards of Nerd Supremacy: The Case of WikiLeaks', *The Atlantic,* 20 December 2010, http://www.theatlantic.com/technology/archive/2010/12/the-hazards-of-nerd-supremacy-the-case-of-WikiLeaks/68217/. The first analysis of the phenomena is Patrice Riemens, 'Some Thoughts on the Idea of "Hacker Culture"', http://cryptome.org/hacker-idea.htm; original article: 'Quelques réflexions sur la "culture hacker"', *Multitudes* 1:8 (2002): 181-187.

72   Jonathan Zittrain, Lawrence Lessig, et al., 'Radio Berkman 171: WikiLeaks and the Information Wars', *MediaBerkman,* 8 December 2010, http://blogs.law.harvard.edu/mediaberkman/2010/12/08/radio-berkman-171/.

73   http://www.YouTube.com/watch?v=JCbKv9yiLiQ.

74   The propagation of the LOIC (Low Orbit Ion Cannon) software, originally a proprietary program to test servers' capacity, was essential for lining up the computer networka necessary to launch DDoS-type of attacks, a kind of voluntary botnet.

need to remain anonymous and the practice of hiding behind the masks of Guy Fawkes, the famous early 17th Century English catholic conspirator – made famous by the comic 'V for Vendetta', is an-other element that illustrates the similarities in method shared between Anonymous and WikiLeaks.

From the perspective of the media, the reaction of the church of Scientology, and that of all Anony-mous victims, was to portray the members of the group as computer fanatics, cyber-terrorists and ultimately dangerous hackers. It is not easy to define Anonymous in terms of ideology, but one aspect cannot escape notice: what is bubbling to the surface from all of the nodes of Anonymous is a very peculiar interpretation of freedom of expression, which is described as 'non-negotiable'.[75] As can be seen with the OpBart operation, Anonymous often appears when censorship shows its face.[76] Anonymous' and WikiLeaks' paths crossed again on December the sixth and tenth, 2010 during Operation Avenge Assange (aka Operation Payback), when several DDoS attacks were mounted, many successful, against a dozen banks and financial institutions which had blocked donations to WikiLeaks.[77]

Exposing the enemy's misdeeds while keeping a mask on, challenging opacity through transpar-ency while remaining anonymous, attacking the powerful actors (churches, armies, governments and banks) through interventions pairing technical competencies with mass media engagement, and adopting an attitude of war or sabotage, are the features Anonymous and WikiLeaks share in common. But the similarities end here. Unlike WikiLeaks, one cannot identify Anonymous with one really existing person because it is does not exist as a singular form but always in plural. In theory, anybody can be part of Anonymous, whereas passing on classified information to WikiLeaks does not result in any affiliation with the person leaking it. Anonymous in its turn, is made up of a great number of individuals, networks, and operations.

Can The Pirate Bay, WikiLeaks and Anonymous be considered as different manifestations of the same hacker spirit? It is clear that the environment that gave birth to Anonymous is, at least par-tially, connected to the high-level world of hacking, as can be seen the from participation of various Anonymous groups to a number of operations conducted by Lulzsec.[78] The hacker motto 'just for fun' finds its expression in the Lulz spirit, which is a transformation of the acronym LOL (Laughing Out Loud), used in online chats. The channel b of 4chan is definitely part of the culture of the first people to call themselves Anonymous, for the simple fact that most of its contents is still posted anonymously.[79] A number of people, arrested during the attempt to suppress Anonymous, were us-ers of 4chan. If you are not familiar or curious about manga, anime, video games, TV series, strange

---

75  An Anonymous member appropriated the notorious phrase 'the American way of life is non-negotiable' from a George W Bush speech where he attempt to justify 'total war against terrorism'.

76  See the video: http://www.YouTube.com/watch?v=MlsLmDOhQ5Y.

77  See Thesis 6 of Geert Lovink, Patrice Riemens, 'Twelve Theses on WikiLeaks,'*Eurozine Magazine,* July 2010. http://www.eurozine.com/articles/2010-12-07-lovinkriemens-en.html.

78  From May to June 2010, the hacker group declared '50 days of Lulz,' hitting targets of various types (FBI, Sony, Fox, Twitter) and also publishing login and password details of users, simply, 'because we can do it'. The pirate vessel of Lulzsec has left a deep mark in the ocean of the Net; the torrent of operations and compromised sites is still available in the mirrors.

79  4chan Showcase was started in 2003 by Christopher Poole (then 15 years old, he managed to stay anonymous till 2008) and takes its inspiration from similar Japanese sites. In early 2011 4chan had the staggering number of more than a half million unique hits a day.

acronyms, black humor, borderline porn, LOLCats (photoshopped cats with captions), culture jamming, etc., then 4chan is definitely not for you. It may seem like a madhouse of macabre and surreal imagery, the meeting place of kids who use incomprehensible terms and the paranoid observer may see it as a breeding ground for cyber terrorists.

The mass media have focused on Anonymous hacking operations, but actually there have been many different types of Anonymous interventions, on multiple networks. There have also been public demonstrations of the more traditional kind, with Anonymous activists donning Guy Fawkes masks. With the politicization of real life actions, Lulz online attacks have become less numerous, and the group became more politically oriented. Until the emergence of groups within Anonymous, who openly called themselves anarchists, for example the A(A)A for Anonymous Anarchist Action. But what kind of anarchism are we talking about here? Is it the anarcho-capitalist variety, bent on the total triumph of the free market, and extreme privatization facilitated by a liberating technology? Or is it anarchy understood as an anti-authoritarian practice and the struggle for a society made up of 'free and equals' individuals, where competition takes a step back for solidarity? Sure, there are members of Anonymous who are active within genuinely anarchist organizations, but there are also among them those who espouse liberal capitalist or even libertarian tendencies. The fact that journalists hailed 4chan as the Web's most anarchist site should raise some doubt. The views of the founder of Moot, the New Yorker Christopher Poole, provide a good benchmark for evaluation. Poole has declared himself in favor of radical opacity, and absolute anonymity online, which give everyone the opportunity to behave 'badly' without worrying about offending, disturbing or being punished. Therefore Pool surely would be opposed to the radical transparency of Facebook. But this is a bit unsubstantial for claiming the subversive anarchist label. Canvas, a site that needs to be authenticated through a Facebook account, is part of the evolution of a showcase format that allows for modification of online images. [80] This is an innovative system for the creation collaborative visual content. But this project is certainly not in the spirit of revolutionary anarchy or anti-authoritarianism. On the contrary, it is a project funded by venture capital, without in any way diverging from the advertisements-based business model already successfully operated by Google, Facebook, and all other Web 2.0 actors extracting profits from digital sociality.

Sociality and politics work in the same way: online practice is narrowly connected with real life practice, and cross-fertilization occurs all the time. Anonymous' initiatives attracted major media attention, which in its turn attracted the unwelcome attention of the police on the group. During the Occupy Wall Street demonstrations, inspired by the occupation of Spanish plazas by the 'Indignados', Anonymous brought in its technical expertise. Twitter and Facebook apps were created to improve communications between protesters. On many occasion, transparency became an defensive weapon against the police, e.g. to identify agents who had beaten protesters. However, the same face identification technology was repeatedly used against the demonstrators themselves. [81]

---

80   See, https://www.facebook.com/canvas.
81   In Rome, after the riots of 15 October 2011, the mass media named and shamed all the suspected Black
     Bloc members. Many could be identified thanks to the help of 'honest citizens'. In another context, and
     on a different scale, the same procedure was used in Iran during the riots of June 2009. The authorities
     requested the participation of citizens to identify the insurgents, who were marked with a red circle on a
     government site. See: http://www.gerdab.ir/fa/pages/?cid=407.

As already mentioned in our discussion of WikiLeaks, practices of informing only work within a democratic context and where a certain amount of liberties and citizen rights still exist, where civil disobedience has a recognized value, and state-sponsored repression rarely endangers the lives of citizens. In all those cases, appeals, claims, and criticism can be much more effective when the actions are carried out in a creative way, like in the examples of Anonymous. However, it is during the construction phase that the inherent weaknesses of mass movements are revealed; yet Anonymous unambiguously claims to be a mass movement by profiling itself as a 'legion' that nothing can stop. To shout out 'Que se vajan todos!' as the Argentinian did in 2001, is a lively equivalent to the methods of digital sabotage but it is still a petition of sorts to the authorities. It asks the ruling powers to loosen their grip, the banks to stop behaving like banks, the governments to stop waging wars and the military to stop killing. All this is legitimate, it is even fair but it is not adequate when considering the concrete reality of these propositions. It is even counterproductive, since the request for change is addressed to the very people who are responsible for repression, and in fact, and in this sense legitimizes their authority in the process. So it is precisely in the construction phase that we should be acutely aware and make a radical shift in perspective. The macroscopic lens of the opposition movement against a corrupt and oppressive power, and proposes alternatives in the name of all is doomed from the start, as it falls within the logic of confrontational which is typical of hegemonic discourse. Once they have had their fun ridiculing banks, churches, corporations and governments, the Anonymous organizers who do not share WikiLeaks' nerd suprematist style, should really start concentrating on the constructive aspects of their technical power. [82] Otherwise, they will end up being co-opted to-morrow by the very powers they ridicule today.

Anonymous' anomaly lies in the fact that its activists hold a great power: the power of technology. They know the intricacies of digital networks and know how to make their existence work to their advantage. They can choose to use this knowledge-power to reinforce the network of already existing organizations. Governments are organizations trying to expand their chances to exercise control, sometime with the benevolent purpose of assistance and aid to the most members of society: in which case they surely need such skills. On the other hand, companies especially the large corporations providing social media services are in desperate need of strengthening their organizations' networks, that is to make them more secure, which means to make them more impenetrable to unwanted elements. But other modes of action are also possible, for instance investing in the organizational capacity of networks in development, which do not have a position to defend, or interests to protect, or copyrighted materials, patents and trademarks but which aim

---

82  Lulz's latest exploits, involving attacks against the security firms Stratfor and SpecialForces.com,
    were highly politicized. Here's what the online press release, LulzXmas, said on December 27, 2011:
    'Continuing the week long celebration of wreaking utter havoc on global financial systems, militaries, and
    governments, we are announcing our next target: the online piggie supply store SpecialForces.com. Their
    customer base is comprised primarily of military and law enforcement affiliated individuals, who have
    for too long enjoyed purchasing tactical combat equipment from their slick and 'professional' looking
    website. What's that, officer? You get a kick out of pepper-spraying peaceful protesters in public parks?
    You like to recreationally Taser kids? You have a fetish for putting people in plastic zip ties?' See Richi
    Jennings, 'Anonymous Antisec hacks STRATFOR in Lulzxmas operation', *Computerworld*, 27 December
    2011, http://www.computerworld.com/article/2471899/cybercrime-hacking/anonymous-antisec-hacks-
    stratfor-in-lulzxmas-operation.html.

to a create a shared systems for exchange and interaction.

In this sense, perhaps the most interesting common trait between Anonymous and Occupy movements is the way they profile themselves as constitutively devoid of leaders and with a strong tendency to self-organization. It is the size of these small organized networks which is the truly innovative aspect of Anonymous and Occupy. The lack of a leader figure or a fixed agenda makes it almost impossible for hierarchical, institutional organizations to engage with such movements. Yet, the Manichean and militaristic caricature of Anonymous as soldiers fighting for the greater good also has to be carefully avoided. Political practices and ideas do not ineluctably arise from the adoption of appropriate technological tools.

# PART III:
# THE FREEDOMS OF THE NET

Any sufficiently advanced technology is indistinguishable from magic.
– Arthur C. Clark

### 3.01 — ONLINE REVOLUTION AND COUCH ACTIVISM: BETWEEN MYTH AND REALITY

The media coverage of the Occupy movement and the logistical and technical support of Anonymous bring us back to considering perspectives and practices of participation, democracy and digital organization. The success commercial social networks have is due to the possibilities of forming and maintaining contacts that is potentially global in extent. However, it is not up to the user to choose how to relate to others, but the service provider which, through exercising 'default power', determines the details of this shared environment. Digital participation assisted by commercial platforms is easier than the commitment required by self-managed analogical organization. The ease of creating a Facebook group to collect funds for refugee or environmental catastrophes etc., is of a totally different order than the resource mobilization required of non-digital, off-line activism. Digital activists feel a false sense of power from being on the net and can conveniently ignore the bureaucracy, dead end group discussion and material problems of their analogical counterparts. The main advantage of armchair activism is that it offers a simulacrum of participation, with 'likes' and 'share this 'link'. The armchair activist can give free reign to their indignation while remaining safe behind their screens, using software produced and managed by tech corporations.

The Western media's enthusiasm for the 'Arab Spring', and the earlier Iranian Green Movement, and others present and future so-called digital movements is the result of the technophilic and internet-centrist perspective we discussed in the first section of this book. At an even deeper level, it reveals a blind faith in information as expression of absolute truth. Activists, and citizens of Western democracies are so ignorant of reality that they are convinced merely removing the cloak of censorship will enable a blossoming of democracy. From this perspective freedom is merely the result of a proper use of appropriate technology, and free information is the host of the democratic gospel. Therefore if the Chinese were allowed to communicate freely, the party leaders would be wiped out, just like the Soviet politburo in 1989. We can always bet on the fact that all coming insurrections will be read through the distorting lens of liberating technology. We should remember Gil Scott-Heron's words: 'you will not be able to stay home, brother.[...] Because the revolution will not be televised'. We have been asked by reporters to comment and analyze digital movements, and our views on Anonymous attacking the IS or similar headlines news – we can only answer: no comment. We do not want in any way legitimize the mythical, militaristic, dualistic (online vs. offline) tale starting with 'once upon a time, the army of Good composed of masked hackers fighting for a better world attacked the armies of Evil'. The Situationists have already explained how The Society of the Spectacle works, we can not help but look for ways of subtraction and desertion.

The technological patina that covers everything these days allows critics to indulge in the same 'cut-and-paste' analysis regardless of social context. According to this view social oppression is the result of communicative misunderstandings and inaccurate information. This is precisely the same discourse of the technocrats who shape communication tools, and develop political marketing strategies. [1] A free society demands an intensification of the circulation of information by accelerating transactions and improving network connections. Here again, technology plays a reassuring role by convincing 'honest citizens in the West' that their attitudes are fine. The sense of emotional closeness that develops in observers who witness acts of repression in real time, helps strengthen the support for the freedom of the people. However, the walls that must fall to achieve this are not technological firewalls, but social, political, and cultural barriers.

The most common objection to the progressive radical critiques of social media technology is that every tool can be put to use in a revolutionary way. However, inside the Facebook aquarium we are constantly bombarded by information stimuli. In this deluge of information, political content is confused with all other subjects, and does not have, nor ever will have, an autonomous space to itself. The relationship of one to many, the illusion of 'spreading the news' at a mouse click has to contend with the white noise of perpetual chatter. The revolutionary event shall be forgotten, buried in the eternal present of digital ephemera, without testimony or memory. Technology is indeed neither good nor evil in itself but must be analyzed in the context of its specific functioning. Technology is power, and power cannot be neutral.

In this sense, Facebook has been extremely successful in realizing it's economic and political project of radical transparency. This technology works when the aims of the users coincide, or at least are compatible, such as in social media marketing, public relations or events planning. But it does not mean that this technology is good in itself. The fact that Facebook and Twitter were used as communication tools during the revolutions in North African 'revolutions' and the uprisings in the Middle East and Asia does not ipso facto transform them into revolutionary devices. People make revolutions not technologies and they rebel by using whatever instruments are at their disposal. In this case rebels used corporate-owned social networks. Each case should be analyzed in a specific fashion: languages, histories and backgrounds are different, territories and populations are distinct and not comparable. If to delve beneath the news about spectacular technology-enabled uprisings, we often discover a much more mundane reality.

In 2011, the West quickly concluded that the Mubarak regime had fallen due to its powerlessness against the popular uprising enabled by the internet. The new wave beginning in Tunisia, was supposed to rapidly spread through the Mediterranean, or at least up to Syria. In reality, the only thing that became clear is that superannuated autocrats like Mubarak were not secure, especially not if they left opposition groups free to galvanize opposition on Facebook for months on end. If we now focus a bit more on the Mediterranean basin, we see no movements in Algeria, whereas a full-blown civil war has erupted in Syria. Meanwhile, Egypt and Tunisia were democratically handing themselves over to extreme Islamist parties, which unlike the previous regimes are far more savvy

---

1    *Spin doctors* are the sophists our time, the professionals of manipulating public opinion. They orchestrate huge campaigns of disinformation to cover up scandals and arrange publicity stunts for the promotion of their clients, usually politicians. A backbone of the US lobby system, *spin doctors* have now started playing an increasingly important role in Europe also. They are a ultimately a byproduct of the development of the advertisement industry and of its logic. If policies are simply products put up for sale, democracy will appear more and more as a Hollywood film or a bad sitcom.

with social media. Libya also appears to be taking the road to Islamic fundamentalism, following a bloody civil war backed by the West for control of oil resources. Its difficult to be optimistic, but commentators continue to be near unanimous in judging the crucial role of social media.[2]

The techno-enthusiastic interpretation of events in Iran is possibly even more disturbing. The vast majority of Farsi tweets posted during the 2009 street protests in Iran, were overseas based Iranian dissidents using their twitter profiles from the safety of the United States or the UK rather than from the streets in Teheran.[3] In April 2010, Moeed Ahmad, Al Jazeera's director, reported

> I believe Twitter has been used far too often, including by news channels which have broadcasted videos and tweets on this issue without first checking the source. We did identify a hundred dependable sources, sixty of which proved really useful. But in the days following the start of the protests only six of them continued to pass on information. I think it is important to realize that on Twitter only 2% of the information is first-hand. All the rest is re-tweeted. So the only strategy where you are going to use social networks purposefully in a journalistic context is to identify the real source of the information and to work with that source only.[4]

We do not very much know yet about how effective Twitter's role was in the Green protest movement in Iran, save that it was doomed to fail from the outset. There is little we can say about the immediate future, as the Iranian theocracy remains in power and taking steps to purge opponents, including on the technological front. Many activists including those who managed to have their voice heard remain skeptical.[5] The fact that there were so many tweets circulating in the West about the revolt in Iran does not mean that many Iranian dissidents were on Twitter. The concrete result was that the Iranian government, monitoring pro-rebel tweets by American and European politicians, brutally censored everybody in Iran who had been in touch with 'Western media', starting a campaign of threats via SMSs and bringing together a special information police force. Bypassing the censorship of social media in Iran has now become a lot more difficult.

Modern securitarian states, in the Middle East and in the rest of the world already exercise control on the two main instruments of power: weapons and money. They are now learning to live with the flow of digital information – as long as this information does not translate into concrete political actions that might threaten the ruling elites. Rami Khouri, foreign correspondent for the Lebanese newspaper Daily Star fears that the global impact of new communication technologies on the political conflicts in the Middle East will ultimately be highly negative. He argues that 'the

2   A collection of sources on the role of social in the Arab spring. https://socialcapital.wordpress. com/2011/01/26/twitter-facebook-and-YouTubes-role-in-tunisia-uprising/.

3   'Oxfordgirl', for instance, was a Twitter user who posted thousands of tweets during this period, sharing informations about the protests. But she is an Iranian journalist based in Oxfordshire, UK.

4   'L'intervento di Moeed Ahmad', *Al Jazeera e i nuevi media,* 27 April 2010, http://www.dailymotion.com/ video/xd3jl5_al-jazeera-e-i-nuovi-media-l-interv_news%20[.

5   'Vahid Online', an Iranian activist blogger who posted from Teheran in 2009 before taking refuge in the United States, stated on several occasions that the influence of Twitter and Facebook inside Iran had actually been near-zero, even though Westerners believed they were actually participating in the uprisings in real-time. See: http://vahid-online.net. Also the blogger Alireza Rezaei pointed out that the chaotic unfolding of the protests did not conform to the idea of a Twitter-organized uprising. See: http:// alirezarezaee1.blogspot.com/.

new media' will function as a mere palliative to the stress of powerlessness rather than an instrument of real change: 'Blogging, reading politically racy Web sites, or passing around provocative text messages by cellphone is equally satisfying for many youth. Such activities, though, essentially shift the individual from the realm of participant to the realm of spectator, and transform what would otherwise be an act of political activism — mobilizing, demonstrating or voting — into an act of passive, harmless personal entertainment.'[6]

So it is all again about spectacles – the spectacles that the authorities allow. Dictatorships are not led by clueless autocrats, easily dislodged by the pressure of free social media. On the contrary, these rulers learn very quickly all what they need to apply technological innovations to their own advantage, to the point that a rebellion which even makes use of these tools becomes dangerous.

The most well organized repressive regimes know how to make use of the same methods as their dissenters; something that yet again demonstrates that technology is not neutral. DDos attacks, one of the one of the 'weapons' popularized by Anonymous was also used by the Saudi government to impose censorship. Philosophy has been banned for years in the Sheiks' universities, since it urges individuals to think for themselves. Western thought is forbidden in Saudi Arabia, furthering the country's schizophrenic position as both a privileged trading partner to Western governments and one of the largest funders of Islamic fundamentalism. In 2006, Tomaar.net was launched by the Saudis to discuss philosophy and share forbidden links and resources which were officially prohibited but still accessible online. Being in Arabic, it had also many non-Saudi followers. But surveillance technology is always improving and it became increasingly easy for the government to trace each visitor of the site. The Saudi government first blocked access to Tomaar from internet terminals in its own territory. Users responded by using anonymization software and anti-censorship proxies. An arm races ensued. The Saudi government launched DDoS attacks against the US server that hosted the forum. Now Tomaar.net is dead.[7] Dissident sites and activist webpages have also been subjected to DDoS attacks from Burma, Belarus, Uzbekistan, Kazakhstan, and Russia. The resulting feeling of powerlessness among dissidents is heightened by the fact that Western government, while eulogizing internet freedom and condemning censorship and repression, still back authoritarian governments through economic, financial and military agreements. This only serves to strengthen such governments at the expense of the very dissidents the West claims to support. We also should not forget that democratic governments also practice censorship, including through DDoS attacks, to prevent their own citizens from accessing content deemed.

Although the role of social media in politics is praised by the Western media, the triumph of democracy is unlikely to be the outcome of corporates-owned technology. In well functioning dictatorships like China, Facebook access is blocked not so much because of the party leaders aversion to radical transparency, but because it is considered as a product of American imperialism. The much criticized collaboration between Google and the NSA in 2010, Google's complaints about attacks from Chinese hackers, Google openly pulling out of China in protest of government censorship, didn't improve things either. Who could blame China for viewing these firms as spies in the pockets

---

6    Rami G. Khouri, 'When Arabs Tweets', *International Herald Tribune,* 22 July 2010, http://www.nytimes.com/2010/07/23/opinion/23iht-edkhouri.html.
7    See: 'Free Speech Case Study: The Demise of Tomaar.net', *Anonymous Proxies,* February 2011, http://www.anonymous-proxies.org/2011/02/free-speech-risks-demise-of-tomaarnet.html.

of Washington? In China, the Facebook, Twitter and Google clones are directly controlled by the government, rather than through the secretive, high-level agreements and collaborations in the United States. In the future the laboratories of consensual dictatorships will greatly improve on this arrangement, and nobody will worry any longer about being on Facebook and Twitter. Everybody will know everything about all the obscene things taking place in public or private – and nothing will change. Anyone will be allowed to become part of the Spectacle. Since everybody will be an accomplice in banality and vulgarity, there will be no more scandals. It is likely that in a near future there will be full cooperation between social media enterprises and governments in the realm of surveillance. In the case of democratic regimes, preventive censorship of users and removal of contents under institutional pressure will be presented as a defense of the common interests against hate speech. In totalitarian regimes, private corporations have zero interest in defending dissidents' anonymity, since that will attract the unwelcome attention of the people in power and such users generally do not generate any substantial advertisement revenue.

The push for transparency, combined with the fragmentation of digital messages and the underlying decrease in attention favors posts that are simplistic sound bites and makes it more difficult to articulate complex arguments or nuanced views. The harsh laws of mass culture are enormously amplified by commercial digital media. Catastrophes get higher view ratings than good news. Crass spectacles and melodrama are more successful than challenging works. After all, what people want is to be entertained rather than challenged. Two millennia ago, Roman emperors already knew that the answer to social strife can be summed up in the famous formula 'panem et circenses '(bread and circuses) where the circuses were bloody massacres between gladiators, wild animals, slaves and opponents of the regime. Today's globalized media circus is played out on television newsreels, blogs, YouTube videos and tweets. It is a convenient and dis-embodied way to experience reality in real time, without any effort, without the dirt and the blood, skimming over the tragedy with our eyes only. Distant tsunamis are explained in plenty of detail, while almost nothing is mentioned about what happens in our immediate surroundings. What is not on Google does not exist; and if you leave no tweet behind, you aren't worth anybody's attention. Even when voyeurism turns into political indignation the protests has barely any notable consequences and is quickly reduced to sterile claims often even before further repression.

Sound policies cannot be expressed in the one hundred and forty characters of an SMS or a microblog. This is equally the case for posts on a Facebook group, and even on a blog, despite the fact that the latter offers more opportunities for interaction. Instead thanks to these formats, sectarian message such as incitement to racial hatred, can rapidly propagate, as was demonstrated with the SMS terror campaigns against ethnic minorities in Nigeria (targeting Christians in 2010) in Kenya 2007, (against Kikuyus) and in Australia in 2005 (against the Lebanese). Somali pirates co-ordinate their operations on Twitter and Mexican drug traffickers glorify the murders they perpetrate on YouTube. Muslim fundamentalist use blogs to praise Sharia law, threaten infidels, execute innocent people, while Neo-Nazis around the world use social media to spread their noxious messages. Western evangelist in favor of internet freedom, particularly social media, perhaps should pay attention to these developments before blinding celebrating internet activism. [8] The

---

8    The Italian artist duo *Liens Invisibles* have created a tool specifically for couch activism. See: http://www.
     lesliensinvisibles.org/2010/05/repetitionr-com-tactical-media-meet-data-hallucination/.

world is far more complex than is shown by the mass media, driven by the logic of the spectacle and advertisement. Yet, as the freedom of speech is eulogized – an abstract freedom devoid of concrete content and knowledge-sharing methodology – at the same time authorities demand more rights to regulate and suppress content by those who think differently, triggering a wave of censorship and surveillance.

## 3.02 — ORWELL, HUXLEY, AND THE SINO-AMERICAN MODEL

Freedom on digital networks is counterbalanced by the demand for greater security, which in turn leads to a demand for more control. The wish to be anonymous is at odds with the will to seek out and prosecute those who threaten social stability. In democratic regimes, this may be pedophiles, serial killers, drug traffickers, terrorists, subversives, etc. The wave of emotions caused by some sensational crime can trigger an irrational response: the passing of laws that violate the most basic civil liberties. But ultimately the potential perpetrator is aware that he is under surveillance. In this sense that he is aware of this, a potential criminal may actually be freer than the rest of the population, which is subjected to an increasingly pervasive digital surveillance and control. Not to mention that fact, which we have already pointed out, that this control does not prevent crime. At most it simply eases the system of punishment, at least in theory, by strengthening the logic the judicial and prison systems.

The pressure to regulate the Web coincides with a demand for more transparency, traceability, and recognition of what is happening in digital worlds. Such requirements also allow for the formation of very heterogeneous social categories. Parents associations are worried about the dangers their children may be exposed to. Lobbies of big media copyright owners (Hollywood, the music industry, publishers) all want to make investigation and removal of protected content easier. Banks wish they could have more effective ways of verifying their account holders' identi-ties in order to reduce online fraud. Harassed ethnic minorities want to find out the identity of their tormentors. Xenophobic nationalists (who, once in power, will give a totalitarian twist to our already security-obsessed democracies) want to identify and register all foreigners in order to vent their frustrations and strengthen their reactionary group identity in ritual pogroms. Victims of violent incidents want to be able to denounce their oppressors without risk of retaliation, by on the one hand protecting their anonymity, while at the same time identifying criminals more effectively through stricter control measures. Outraged citizens want to see the income tax returns of corrupt politicians published so as to name and shame them in the media. Even au-thoritarian regimes like more transparency since they want to keep a close eye on their citizens. Transparency increases the opportunities for surveillance and that makes it desirable to almost all political powers.

The 20th century saw two major dystopias profoundly influence Western thought in the matter of surveillance: George Orwell's Big Brother in his novel 1984' (1949) and Aldous Huxley's 'Brave New World' (1932, followed in 1958 'Brave New World Revisited'). Both authors represent oppo-site dystopias: Orwell, the Englishman, was worried about total 'optical' control, whereas Huxley – English born, but writing from the California – saw an upcoming emotional lobotomy generated by unbridled consumerism.

For Orwell, the emergence of totalitarian systems marked a new phase, reminiscent of the Inqui-sition, in which technology was used to abolish the privacy of citizens. The omnipresent eye of Big

Brother's exercises a power that is both sadistic and oppressive. Big Brother is able to change reality itself through Newspeak, the language specifically designed to limit the range of possible expressions. Every personal move must be completely predictable, and everybody must obey. The protagonist in '1984', Winston Smith, discovers that neurologists working for the regime are attempting to eliminate orgasm, in order to completely suppress desire, that dangerous moment of psychophysical instability, which could potentially trigger revolt.

In Huxley's vision, technology, on the contrary, is used to maximize pleasure, as part of a cycle of continuous consumption. In the world of Huxley's Fordist consumerism, throwing away is preferable to repairing, and citizens have no incentive whatsoever to think in an autonomous and critical way, since their pleasures find satisfaction even before having been formulated. Of course, not everyone's desires are identical: a rigid system of castes, from 'Alphas' to 'Epsilons', is managed through eugenic control. Different categories of consumers exist, which are preassigned to consume specific goods and services. But desire is diminished through excess with a system of compulsory sexual promiscuity. Family bonds are deemed pornographic because they are privileged links. Social interactions are organized in a fully transparent way, to the extent that women are forced to wear a contraceptive belt, which signals their immediate sexual availability. Individuals are consumer goods like any other, must express who they are without ambiguity.

With Orwell, there is a higher level of conspiracy in which some freedom is possible, at least among the oppressors. In the world of Huxley, nobody is free, not even the 'Alphas'. They too must perform their duties of daily consumption, just like those they command. Conformity is the supreme good, docile obedience is necessary to have the entire population reduced to a state of infantile bliss. A daily dose of the drug 'Soma' and hypnopedia (indoctrination during sleep) wards off such mortal sins as the desire for solitude, autonomy and independence.

It is precisely these forbidden desires that we will have to return to in order to imagine a new expression of social networks. The only way to escape induced desires and conformity is the rejection of social performance. One cannot deny that both Orwell's fearful dystopia and Huxley's enforced entertainment provide insights into our own contemporary societies. Evgeny Morozov stresses our tendency to underestimate the number of Orwellian elements in democratic regimes (with the reality TV show 'Big Brothers' the fear of control has become a joke) while at the same time discounting the Huxleyan elements present in dictatorships. Most dictators prefer to distract and entertain the masses rather than dominate them with terror, because in the long term overt repression tends to generate violent riots. Hedonistic consumerism on the other hand, may strengthen consent, or at least gain some acceptance from the oppressed.

Better yet, 'panem et circenses' politics may even encourage the masses into supporting a despotic regime. Why should a Chinaman, a Turk or a Cuban not praise the government in exchange for some gift? Ultimately, the internet does bring to many authoritarian societies exactly the type of entertainment people need to escape from their disappointing reality: pornography, gossip, innocuous TV series, quizzes, gambling, video-games, online dating and government supervised discussion forums. In fact, this is also exactly the same type of entertainment that allows citizens in democratic societies to escape from their daily reality. Naomi Klein correctly points out marked similarities that exist between China and the West (and more specifically, between China and the United States), a successful combination of Orwellian control and Huxleyan distraction: 'China is becoming more like us in very visible ways (Starbucks, Hooters, cellphones that are cooler than ours), and we are becoming more like China in less visible ones (torture, warrantless wiretapping, indefinite detention, though not nearly on the Chinese scale).' [9]

Profiling techniques used by Google, Facebook, and others can be applied to improve the relevance of individually targeted advertisements just as it can be used to refine individually targeted censorship and repression. If your friends are fans of a certain band, chances are that you will like this kind of music too, and are a potential customer by association. And if your friends read the same subversive blog as you do, then they too are potential dissidents, just like you. The algorithms used to arrive at these results are precisely the same. The Chinese and American social formats have in common the drive towards increased transparency. The Clinton administration in the nineties was failed in its attempt to realize the 'information superhighway', but nothing proves that the Chinese Communist Party may not be successful in its attempts to create a great Peoples' Republic. With assistance from the American military-industrial complex, China is busy creating the prototype of a high-tech police state. The plan is to give every Chinese citizen an email account, a profile on government-owned social networks, an account for online purchase on authorized sites, and storage space to store personal data on regime servers. A kind of nationalized, Chinese Facebook, integrated into a Chinese email, storing data on the Chinese iCloud, and able to suggest what to purchase next from the Chinese clone of Amazon. This scenario highlights the fact that the policies of the IT giants, and especially of those which require ever more sophisticated profiling to boost their profitability – as is the case with the four largest: Facebook, Google, Apple, and Amazon – is totally compatible with authoritarian control systems. These technologies correspond perfectly to the needs of modern dictatorships.

The general acceptance of this profiling is what makes the coming of this social model possible. Chinese authoritarian capitalism, proves perfectly reconcilable with American democratic capitalism. Indeed, the two systems actually support each other. From a financial perspective they are totally interdependent, since the Chinese sovereign wealth funds includes a large part of America's public debt, and thus China could, given the amount of its US Dollar reserves, destabilize Washington. From the economic point of view, American high-tech companies could never amass the kind of extraordinary profits they make without low-cost industrial inputs from China. To take just one example if iPods, iPhones and iPads were manufactured in the West rather than in the industrial district of Shenzhen, their cost would be astronomical. The FoxConn factory workers, who put together these alluring objects of desire, are forced to sign contracts in which they pledge not to commit suicide, an event which is not uncommon, given the inhuman working conditions. Business practices that these workplaces depend on would be impossible to implement in Western countries.

Both these systems share a need to more effectively identify their own population. The United States must supply consumer goods in order to guarantee the happiness written in the social contract while at the same time detecting and neutralizing potentially subversive threats to the system. China needs to improve the material life conditions of the people without allowing the development of democratic politics, at the same time it needs to restrain ethnic and religious tensions. Unlimited growth is of course the basis common to both approaches. The rest of the world,

---

9    Naomi Klein, 'China's All-Seeing Eye', *Rolling Stone Magazine*, 14 May 2008, http://www.naomiklein. org/articles/2008/05/chinas-all-seeing-eye.

meanwhile, does not sit still, and every country participates as much as it can in this competition. Some countries go for the Orwellian approach, others prefer a more sophisticated model with subtle profiling, the Huxleyan way. The social network thus morphs into a trap where flat individualities, also known as pancake people, split up by profiling, trash around. At that stage it becomes increasingly challenging to convince these people to buy stuff because they are not even able to consume a fraction of what they have already accumulated, while they produce extraordinary amounts of industrial waste. They waddle around in search of personalized commodities, passive entertainment and collective identities.

## 3.03 — ON ANTHROPOTECHNICS: REACTION AND SURVIVAL

Not all is lost, it is possible to remove data and to vanish from commercial social networks. We can ignore the revelations from WikiLeaks' for what they are, and in the meanwhile build up alternatives free from control, like Lorea, the Diaspora Project or OpenLeaks. [10] It is possible to build profiling-free search engines, cloud computing services, and more general communication networks that are owned and managed by the users themselves. In the spirit of curiosity, typical of the hacker, we could start make it building physical networks for autonomous communications. Everything is within reach, and independent tools are a more desirable option than to outsource digital sociality to private companies. But at the same time, we need to realize that no alternative is going to be totally free. Even if we manage to define in concrete terms what it means to be free, and are able to mobilize the necessary energies, the most difficult task still remains: to the actual construction of new tools. The challenge is not to rebel for the sake of rebelling, but to imagine ways to develop autonomy and to put these into practice, here and now.

The first method to escape the effects of radical transparency is the adoption of encryption and anonymization tools. Any encrypted email is unreadable for whoever does not possess the appropriate decryption key. All searches we perform on the internet can also be anonymized, as well as our connection to computer networks and data stored on our computers, and smartphones. There are very powerful hybrid encryption algorithms available, such as GPG (Gnu Private Guard). [11] Anonymous web browsing is possible, through making use of software such as TOR, a system first developed by the US Navy, but now an independent project. [12] TOR allows

---

10   Lorea is a self-managed, autonomous social network. See: http://lorea.org/.

11   In asymmetric cryptography, every actor involved holds two keys, a public key, and a private one. The public key can be distributed (or public on a repository) and is used to encode a document that is sent to a receiver who holds the corresponding private key. The private key is individual and secret and is used to decrypt a document that has been encrypted with a public key. In other words everybody can send us a message, encoded with our public key, but only we can open it. With symmetric cryptography, on the other hand, there is only one key and one code. GPG is a free software project using exclusively non-patented algorithms. As prescribed by the OpenPGP charter, it is a hybrid system, where each message is encoded with a symmetric key, used for that message only, which is in turn encoded with the receiver's public key. See: https://www.gnupg.org/. Various plugins are available for easy OpenPGP to add-on to email clients, such as Enigmail: https://www.enigmail.net/home/index.php.

12   Each TOR node negotiates asymmetric keys with other nodes. In this way the overall security of the network increases with the total number of nodes connected because analysis and decryption becomes increasingly difficult if not impossible. To properly use TOR you can download a browser already configured specifically for anonymous surfing directly from the project site. See: https://www.torproject.org/.

users to hide their requests by connecting them, first to intermediary nodes (proxies) or to other randomly selected TOR nodes, from where they finally reach their desired site. Protecting your privacy whenever possible is always a good idea. The use of cryptographic instruments should be the rule, not the exception.

It is also advisable to become more familiar with our everyday tools. However, one should always keep in mind that protection is always relative, never absolute, but provides a reasonable level of security with regard to the current state of technology. With sufficient financial resources and computing power, decoding an encrypted communication is only a matter of time. As far as anonymization is concerned, blocking of proxies is always an option in a system of diffuse surveillance: we have seen that this practice exists both in democratic and in authoritarian states. If the user has been marked as dangerous by the surveillance system, the use of physical coercion is always another option. But the most counter-productive aspect of these technologies is that in a world where everybody trusts everybody else, and use their real name in digital interactions, those who behave different and use encryption or anonymization are assumed to have something to hide. The simple fact of using these systems make us self-evident targets. Similarly not having a Facebook account or a mobile phone arouses suspicion in others.

Cryptography is not easy to use, and requires a reasonable level of technical competence, which is a major obstacle to its widespread adoption. As a specialized form of knowledge power, cryptography reinforces the emergence of a hierarchy of more or less trustworthy experts. Also, it does not really protect against profiling, since it is perfectly possible to profile users of cryptography, as soon as they communicate with less wary users: by tracing the group 'fingerprint' it is possible to reconstruct the history of user out. The paradox being that the more I try to protect myself, the more I stand out from the crowd, and hence become increasingly more recognizable. If your browser uses extensions to prevent profiling and enables anonymization and encryption, and if your operating system is of a particular type like GNU/Linux, you become much more visible to prying electronic eyes than a user with less sophisticated and more 'mainstream' systems. [13]

Finally cryptography has attracted a lot of criticism by those who consider that it shares the same idea of unlimited growth – always increasing speed and power – as libertarian turbo-capitalism. The increase in computing power and accelerating network speed, increases the effectiveness of the latest cryptographic systems: but this also rapidly renders older systems obsolete. This dynamic of innovation-obsolescence is reminiscent of military confrontation, with a logic of attack and defense, espionage and counterespionage. We should recall that these were systems that were originally designed for military purposes and that they were intended to prevent communication interception by the enemy. Ultimately, encryption is a good practice, especially for technology geeks who enjoy logical puzzles, but its basic approach is not satisfactory.

---

13   The *Panopticlick* project of the Electronic Frontier Foundation: https://panopticlick.eff.org provides not only a way to examine the search engine one uses, but also demonstrates how digital fingerprints in email and social media are used and what we can do to prevent this. EFF's initiative also points out that those who excel the most in their use of digital tools are the most easily detectable. An explanation of the methodology used can be found in the article: Peter Eckersley, 'How Unique is Your Web browser?', *Proceeding PETS'10 Proceedings of the 10th International Conference on Privacy Enhancing Technologies*, Springer, 2010, https://panopticlick.eff.org/browser-uniqueness.pdf.

The second common reaction, which is especially tempting for those who detest hacking culture, is Luddism. The Luddite is convinced that information and communication technologies should be completely rejected or even destroyed. Their reasons include the fact that these technologies are a threat to personal and collective liberties, they provide democratic or authoritarian governments formidable instruments of repression and they tend to create structures of technocratic domination. In fact there are both technophobe and technophile luddites. The former are more consistent with themselves, they are not at ease with appliances, especially digital ones. They often idealize a mythical, natural past world, which never existed, where humans were free from the yoke of machines. Their mantras are 'things were better before' or 'in the past this would never have happened'. They are not entirely mistaken: Ivan Illich's criticism of industrial technology tools is still relevant today. Technical systems become counter-productive when they develop beyond a certain point, and once they have passed the threshold of usefulness, they become harmful. Cars within cities are a slow, polluting and dangerous means of transport. The same appears to be true of the social internet, which more and more resembles a system that makes us feel alone while being in company, with everybody being individually connected to the big network without physical contact with the other people on it.

But the technophobic luddite is not consistent in his desire for nature-based purity; human history is cultural history, made up from the development of technical ideas, which become materialized in technological tools. The problem resides in domination practices, not in technology itself, which does no more exist anymore than the concept of nature in itself does. The most extremist luddites advocate the destruction of all technical systems. Anarcho-primitivists like John Zerzan, for example, would like to abolish not only the internet, but also agriculture, art, language, all being considered tools of oppression. But who wants to live in such a world? Fundamentalist luddites worship the inviolability of nature, and are fanatics in the religious sense of the term: they even promote the total extinction of the human race as the sole remedy to the impending catastrophe. [14]

Technophile luddites have a rather more schizophrenic attitude. They appreciate the convenience and opportunities offered by technological developments, especially those that bring them in contact with others. But they refuse to take an interest in the way these social networking tools actually work. They make no effort to understand, self-manage or tweak these technologies, since it is so much easier to outsource these problems. They have great confidence in the experts and call them up as soon as they encounter a problem. With this type of careless behavior they contribute to the emergence of technocracy. This does not prevent them from complaining bitterly

14    For an excellent refutation of the absurd logic of extinctionalist nihilism csee the article: Marco Maurizi, 'Che cos' è l'antispecismo', *Liberazioni*, no 4, February 2008, http://www.liberazioni.org/articoli/ MauriziM-06.htm. Note 7 reads: 'Extinctionism is utter nonsense because of its absurdity from a purely logical point of view. If humanity could gain collective awareness of their own radical evil and ultimately choose to self-annihilation, it would mean we have achieved such a high moral level that it would call into question this very evil and in fact we would become the most altruistic animal ever seen on the face of the earth! So it is either the case that humanity can consciously speed up their own extinction (and then all the more reason to think that we are able to accomplish ethical feats of a very different nature), or not (in which case the entire movement for voluntary extinction is meaningless). Obviously those who flirt with the idea of extinction mostly do so for the sake of provocation. But then I cannot see the point of this provocation, since it prevents any sensible analysis of the relationship between nature and society.'

that they do not understand anything about these irksome devices and to furiously attack the experts when they realize that nobody is going to manage their instruments free of charge and that even experts are not able to solve their problems once and for all.

Perhaps the most common practice is to deliberately embrace technocracy and to and to surrender to outsourcing problems. It is natural, when bombarded with contradictory messages and the chaos of information, to think that these issues are so huge that they can be resolved independently. The internet is global and some digital technologies are more pervasive than others. The technological patina that covers everything makes us believe that the problem is universal. Techno-enthusiast argue that to manage this knowledge independently because human beings are by nature selfish and greedy, ready to go to war. They believe in Hobbes' famous dictum, that man is a wolf to his fellow man. For the greater good, it is better to delegate to some capable figure and overcome the typical human inadequacies. Technophiles believe that it is necessary to setup institutions and organizations responsible for addressing these technological issues, and preferably at a global scale. These organizations should ensure citizens' liberties and rights, and of course an adequate level of consumerism.

Technocracy is inherently scientific and it is difficult to oppose without being accused of obscurantism, opposition to progress, or simple naivety. Technocrats want to regulate every aspect of the internet through setting up systems of control. These technocrats are therefore in favor of expanding the panoptic model. Within the Matrix, users live under the guidance of experts forming the disembodied great collective intelligence, a society of total knowledge, a kind of fantasy replica of Teilhard de Chardin's 'noosphere'. [15] Technocratic extremism finds its realization in the post-humanist and transhumanist movements; but even the moderates demanding global regulation of the internet actually contribute to the advancement of radical transparency and global profiling.

The assumption underpinning the technocratic position is that technologies are inherently good and the outcome of scientific objective and disinterested research. The machines do not lie because they are not capable of lying and would have no interest in doing so. This may be the case, but let us not forget that machines are programmed by humans, who have many personal interests at stake, and they are perfectly capable of lying, even to themselves. Technocracy

---

15   Pierre Teilhard de Chardin (1881-1955) uses the term noosphere to describe the stage of human
     evolution when the earth will be enshrouded in a layer of interconnected thinking, just before the advent
     of Cosmic Christ, or Omega Point. Teilhard de Chardin's futurology- and technological mysticism has
     a large influence on transhumanist movements. The Roman Catholic hierarchy was initially opposed
     to Teilhard de Chardin, but he was subsequently rehabilitated by Pope Benedict XVI (formerly Jozeph
     Cardinal Ratzinger), who in a vesper homily at the Aosta cathedral on July 24, 2009 said that 'St Paul's
     vision is the great vision that was also shared by Teilhard de Chardin: in the end we shall have a truly
     cosmic liturgy, and the Cosmos shall become a living Host'. See: John L. Allen Jr., 'Pope Cites Teilhardian
     Vision of the Cosmos as a 'Living Host', National Catholic Reporter, 28 July 2009, http://ncronline.
     org/news/pope-cites-teilhardian-vision-cosmos-living-host. Eric S. Raymond is also at home in the
     noosphere and believes hackers are simply colonizing it. See his essay: Eric S. Raymond, 'Homesteading
     the Noosphere', The Cathedral & the Bazaar, California: O'Reilly, 1999, http://www.catb.org/esr/
     writings/homesteading/homesteading. The spiritual noosphere is the future point of convergence for the
     Roman Catholic Church and anarcho-capitalism.

is based on the delegation of technological knowledge-power to others. With the absence of mechanisms of shared delegation, hierarchies tend to be structured in an authoritarian manner and to lose touch with their historic background, which is the outcome of social conventions and agreements. There is a large difference between acknowledging the authority of someone as a competent person in a certain field and giving this person a mandate, which is verified regularly and revocable, to blind trust in the supremacy of a technocrat. In the latter case the experts-priests' power becomes unassailable and unquestionable. Naturally, it will always be presented as redeeming, and this often in millenarian terms; if you do not choose the right technician, you are lost. [16] The IT expert, even more than a medical doctor, is the shaman of our contemporary age. Will my computer recover from this virus that infected it? Is there any hope for recovering the data I lost? The authority of the expert leads to the paradoxical situation in where every action becomes a request to the principle of an external authority, and simultaneously, a statement of self-disparagement. First we have to confess to our own ignorance and inadequacy, make amend for past errors and humbly ask for assistance, only to discover that experts are not at all custodians of objective knowledge. Sometimes these disappointed techno-enthusiasts can become disillusioned technophile luddites.

Technolatry is the inevitable consequence of technocracy. Technology becomes an idol to worship. Confidence turns into faith, and into the belief that there exist miraculous solutions that will solve social problems. We expect technical solutions to a whole range of problems like pollution, global warming, world hunger and new, fanciful mythologies are being devised: green fuels, clean technology and genetically modified crops. These quick fixes to pressing problems are almost magical. Like any hegemonic apparatus, technocracies dull critical capacity as they demand blind collaboration from people and claim a range of identities in, a social chain without apparent beginning or end. Everything is connected because everyone is involved and no one can opt out. All forms of consumerism, and especially those inspired by techno-enthusiasm, are tributes to technocracy. They confirm that there is no alternative to the present system, because they avidly buy the latest gadget put on the market as the magic key to happiness. Personal desire has been expropriated by advertising itself and is now reduced to the predatory search for the best deal. As then individual ever more transparent, technical mediation progresses in an increasingly opaque way, making the development of knowledge-power totally impenetrable. Technocratic society is the society of Mega Machines, in which nobody is responsible, but where everybody is a tiny cog in the global mechanism – at least as a consumer. The top of the hierarchy is just as elusive as its bottom, and to escape the system is simply inconceivable. [17]

---

16   A striking example of this taking place in Italy is the phrase 'a technical government', which describes the government that was formed in November 2011 and made up of experts not coming from politics but entrusted with the task to save the country.

17   The criticism of techno-bureaucracies can easily be applied to the domination of the IT sphere, which Donna Harraway denounces in 'A Cyborg Manifesto, Science, Technology, and Socialist-Feminism in the late Twentieth Century' in *Simians, Cyborgs, and Women: the Reinvention of Nature*, New York: Routledge, 1991, p. 161. Available at: http://www.egs.edu/faculty/donna-haraway/articles/donna-haraway-a-cyborg-manifesto. Aggregative hierarchic systems have a tendency to develop coercive social formats, irrespective of the time period. The personal competencies required to function in such systems are inversely proportional to technical skills. See the analysis of the Soviet power system in Cornelius Castoriadis, *La Societé bureaucratique*, Paris: Bourgois, 1990.

Peter Sloterdijk asserts in 'Rules for the Human Zoo' that, what he calls, humanistic anthropo-technics is in crisis. [18] The project to breed and train citizens through public education has col-lapsed, the project to develop mass literacy could be replaced by eugenics to engineer are more civilized race. There is no need to resort to genetic engineering; social engineering is already more than enough. We have already seen how the use of invasive social technologies leads to automated forms of obedience which are then portrayed as necessary and beneficial. Observing this process, we can easily detect the anthropotechnics of Facebook. In this way, the biopolitical control of both bodies and minds is decentralized as much as possible towards the individual, who becomes answerable for her own subjugation to technology. The transparent individual already lives outside of herself, in the technological sphere, and no longer has any secrets or any other space to retreat to. Such an individual increasingly loose confidence in their autonomy because they have become less competent, and they surrender to the incomprehensible vastness of the global network. It seems for them that there is no longer any way to make things work.

Finance is a good illustration of this type of mechanism, where the mouse click of amateur investors and uncontrollable forces are capable of wiping our entire economies. Technocracies themselves are portrayed as the rational solution to all social problems, but in fact they are ultimate expression of the irrationality of the economy. Anthropocentrism tends to lead us into believing in a rational intentionality present behind every event, so it becomes obvious to see a correlation between the uncontrollable power of technology and natural forces, something made near-explicit in everyday language, with terms like 'financial tsunami', information deluge, innova-tion waves, etc. Merging technology with nature results in attitudes bordering on mysticism and produces absurd vacillations between the will to power and the desire to rebel. The perfect indi-vidual within a global technocratic regime is docile and apathetic. Obedient to the rules decreed and by her enthusiastic, defeatist or passive attitude, she forces potential rebels to conform. Such an individual is neither a charismatic leader nor an exceptional figure, but a supporter of technical banality, in other words a little Eichmann of contemporary techno-totalitarianism. In the words of Lewis Mumford: 'In every country there are now countless Eichmanns in administrative offices, in business corporations, in universities, in laboratories, in the armed forces: orderly, obedient peo-ple, ready to carry out any officially sanctioned fantasy, however dehumanized and debased.' [19]

### 3.04 — BEYOND THE NET OF EMPTY NODES: AUTONOMOUS INDIVIDUALS AND ORGANIZED NETWORKS

Becoming a member of a commercial social network costs nothing. Therefore, digital involvement has become an integral part of the global spectacle. The underlying issue, once again, is the ar-ticulation of individual and collective identity. Just like relationships that require zero effort, identi-ties that have zero value fall apart at the first gush of wind. This of course costs, only in terms of necessary skills, invested time, and a passion to share something, not in terms of money. In more

---

18    Peter Sloterdijk, 'Rules for the Human Zoo. A Response to the Letter on Humanism', *Environment and Planning D: Society and Space*, 27 (2009): 12-28, http://rekveld.home.xs4all.nl/tech/Sloterdijk_RulesForTheHumanZoo.pdf.

19    Lewis Mumford, *The Pentagon of Power: The Myth of the Machine, Vol. II*. New York: Harcourt Brace Jovanovich, 1970, p. 279.

'Huxleyan' societies, where consumerism is the task of every citizen, not only goods, but also the social groups to which people belong, signal their social status. Digital activism, more often than not is a way to impress friends rather than to realize deeply held political convictions. Membership of special interests groups is also largely brought about by narcissism, need for self-promotion, and the requests for attention that are manifest in the creation of personal profiles.

This dynamic is not new and is not exclusive to digital networks. Impressing peers by defending noble causes, such as protesting against a genocide going on in a remote country or campaigning to save baby seals, is one of the many ways to understand social commitment. Analog activism is corrupted by this same phenomenon of group fetishism which draws an individual into participating in as many groups as possible, following more training courses, committing themselves to any cause that presents itself, only to suffer information overload and feel deflated. The real driving force however if often a lack of personal identity coupled with a need to feel part of a larger whole, a collective identity that gives meaning to the exhausted single person. We now will focus our attention on this individual subject, the hero of the free market cheered on by anarcho-capitalists. As Castoriadis points out, privatization has nothing to do with individualization. We need true, different individuals, not interchangeable atoms. The individual subject is not a rational given, realized in a single identity, but a permanent ongoing process, shaped by her relationships with the surrounding environment.

In the era of profit maximization, co-operation among free people who respect each other may seem like an obsolete idea. Not to mention friendliness; who still has the time, or wish, to comfortably chat, make plans, be creative or simply spend time with like-minded people? Setting up a place of conviviality has nothing to do with becoming members of a group supporting some common cause without direct face-to-face contact. Conviviality presupposes the existence of a stable 'we' that would be at least able to tell its own history, to represent and to take care of itself by building up collective spaces and sharing common moments of life. But now, when it corresponds to something more than a generic 'like', as soon as it is not in the service of some identity-based reactionary statement, the pronoun 'we' becomes almost an insult. It evokes a community in the old-fashioned sense, the provincialism of small quarrels. It is far better to deal with gossip and to 'manage' a mass of non-demanding contacts, than to waste time with just a few interpersonal relationships.

It is a very flat 'me' that takes the center stage in the performance society. The successful 'me' does not need strong ties with any particular community. All that is required is personal ambition, sustained by appropriate skills, e.g. the ability to sell oneself well. These personal resources have been accumulated during the continuous disruptions the self has experienced and adjusted to during our working life: corporate restructuring, work overload and stress, followed by periods of forced inactivity and lifelong learning. The time outside of work reflects perhaps and even greater degree of structural instability, with serial relocations to 'seize the right opportunity', and friendships maintained on Facebook or by instant messaging. These are the experiences that have shaped the flexible 'me'. No wonder then if, after thirty years of 'weak ties', angst, euphoria and depression follow each other in quick succession. 'Holiday' is not a valid concept in our performance society.

The internet, which enables this type of flexibility, is also the favorite metaphor of the gurus of mass participation, who praise flexibility as the universal cure for social ills, and also for those who pontificate on the endless opportunities of the digital. Today's managers love to use terms like 'networking', 'decentralization', 'horizontal', 'interconnected', 'outsourcing', 'crowd-funding', as if networks have the sole goal of raising profits and lowering costs.

But there is a big difference between 'networked organizations' and 'organized networks'. A hierarchical organization can benefit from networking, because removing some power from the top and distributing responsibilities can help leverage employees' passions, appealing to their sense of belonging in the group and their sense of autonomy. Flexible capitalism still remains hierarchical and authoritarian, but uses 'networks' with bonuses and back-scratching recreating the false sense of an otherwise disparaged 'we'.

Free networking platforms are the latest invention of capitalism to enhance productivity. Each and every minute spent on corporate social media is actually work time. Users are rewarded for their continuous activity with complimentary services. While LinkedIn and similar services are explicitly used for professional life, Facebook is also used for work-related activities. It is a kind of office where we are all guests, full of entertainment that serves to make us spend more time at work. It comes as no surprise that a lot of marketing applications are developed and launched on social media, the aim being to combine production networks with kinship ones, with the merging of the two as the ultimate aim. But it is important to at least enjoy sometime not working and free from the imperative of constant productivity. Furthermore, there is a psychic wage.

In reality the majority of time spent on so-called networking is made up of 'down-time', misunderstandings and attempts at reconciling, or at least managing the differences that arise from conflicts. [20] In short, most a network is not productive unless it is hierarchically organized. Decentralized and autonomous networks on the other hand, are neither suitable for work, nor for unlimited growth. A networked organization may be more productive but an autonomous network will not since it does not distribute resources in a market-efficient way, especially when the entire relationship interface is virtual. Digital mediated collaboration is challenging and often tiresome if there is never any meeting in real life'. Online work can be extremely inefficient and slow because it requires more listening and patience than work done offline.

In addition to this, and contrary to networked organization which can count on solid and well-established links with technocratic structures, autonomous networks encounter great difficulties in getting recognized by institutions. This is the case with entire sectors like literature, the arts, and academic research. Participatory science is an area of great interest for the development of collaborative dynamics. We are not talking here about sharing one's computer or bandwidth for the benefit of astronomic or genetic research, but to take real interest in the world around us. People curious and passionate about a specific topic could collaborate with experienced scientists and academics to develop a rigorous study that would still be intelligible to the non-initiated. Experts, confined in their specialist knowledge, are rarely able to express themselves in a simple

---

20   The phatic function, in Roman Jakobson analysis of communication, is used to establish contact and verify that the communication channel is not broken. Saying 'Hello' when picking up the phone is a phatic function. All preliminary arrangements that need to be made when calling a group meeting with its complex communication requirements (arranging a venue, making up the agenda, etc.) are similar to the phatic function. When groups make use of digital technologies, verification of the systems often take much more time than in 'analog' situations.

but non-trivial way. Often, for these experts, sharing this knowledge amounts to giving away their hard-earned knowledge. Conversely, the curious non-expert, who does not have a position at stake, could translate the discourse of their expert friends, making a complicated issue more approachable. Naturally, this translation of specialists jargon into a language more accessible to a lay audience risks a certain amount of approximations and simplification, but this is necessary for widespread scientific education. [21] For this reason, the process of building a shared knowledge should be made transparent. Genuine participation requires interested people being directly involved in the process of spreading knowledge.

In politics, this fact is even more obvious. The Indignados movement, Occupy and Anonymous show once more than institutions really hate to dealing with amorphous structures, without (explicit) leaders and hierarchy, because, from their point of view, when nobody is responsible then everyone is. [22] In which case it becomes easy to approach the institution under a false pretense, by devising a fake identity, as an association, etc. Yet for an autonomous network, the bureaucratic burden associated with a public identity is a heavy one. Who wants to go through all the administrative and financial bureaucracy just to obtain public recognition? The alternative then is to cast a leading individual, who can pass of the creation of the group as their own. This is the WikiLeaks approach: one person claims to be responsible, the author or leader, so the media have a 'success story'. For this scenario to work, mutual trust is essential, and it still remains a double-edged sword, especially for organized networks with a radical orientation. This is because, in these radical organizations, the person cast as the leader is likely to be targeted by the authorities or become a notorious figure in the public eye.

Finally, if an autonomous networks wishes to maintain a really horizontal organization without flattening out, it cannot grow beyond a certain limit. To maintain the empowerment that comes from varied work, every participant needs to be heard, with the consequence that the number of 'human nodes' must remain relatively low. This means it is unlikely that these autonomous groups will achieve the critical mass required to be considered proper movements. But these groups generally have to become hegemonic. They do not make use of advertising techniques since even the most subversive publicity stunt will immediately be recycled by the society of the spectacle. Instead, they are more concerned about each other, their relationships and their projects.

---

21   Beatriz da Costa, 'Amateur Science: A Threat After All?', 2005, http://rixc.lv/reader/txt/txt.
     php?id=149&l=en and Brian Martin, 'Grassroots Science', Sal Restivo (ed.), *Science, Technology, and
     Society: An Encyclopedia*, Oxford: Oxford University Press, 2005, pp. 175-181, http://www.bmartin.cc/
     pubs/05Restivo.html.
22   In fact, this impossibility to assign responsibilities is the real reason for the massive occurrence
     of networked, virtual interface organizations. The call centers tasked with monitoring consumer
     satisfaction are the most blatant example: if your internet connection is broken, you phone a call
     center for assistance, where nobody is actually responsible for the failure of the connection. It will
     always someone's else fault: for instance another company did the cable-laying, etc. Hence, networked
     organizations present themselves to users as if they had no leadership, as if they were for all practical
     purposes amorphous structures, where nobody is answerable (especially when they go bankrupt)
     whereas they are, for the institution which finance and own them, very reliable and well-structured.

The time of the autonomous network is a time non-work and non-productivity.[23] It is free and freedom is not productive. Freedom can be creative in certain circumstances. But then it is essential that each node in the network is as autonomous as possible. Nodes need to be competent and therefore relevant to other nodes but also keen to share. This the exact opposite of Huxley's Brave New World of obedient citizen. Socialbots will not be able to infiltrate an autonomous organized network, the way they do on social media, at least as long as it remains impossible to reduce every members to their digital profile.

Conversely, social networks like Facebook's are the ultimate example of network capitalism, which manages to make even the time spent on playing Farmville productive. When playing in the digital space offered by Facebook we are not engaged in a creative activity, but rather an activity that creates more profits through profiling. By participating in the mass construction of a privately owned world, we become mere guests who get their work tools for free.

The conversion of libido into profit is a process that already began a long time ago. There is a sort of psychic wage one can earn by using connected digital tools. Proponents of the gift economy on the internet always neglect to mention that the real gift is the one that users bring everyday by spending their time on the platforms of private companies who profit from their data. A gift that perhaps millions of individuals are quite unaware of but that has enormous economic value. They become mere biomass to fuel the myth of unlimited growth.

## 3.05 — MASS PARTICIPATION

The most well known example of mass collaboration is Wikipedia, the universal encyclopedia, now numbering several million entries in dozens of languages, and which was created by the contributions of millions of volunteers worldwide. It is a astounding experiment, that has many innovative features compared to traditional participatory models. It is also unique that as one of the most widely visited websites on the net, it does not finance itself through advertisements, but depends exclusively on donations. Wikipedia's principal virtue lies in the fact that it puts special emphasis on the non-economic incentives which inspire web users to collaborate on a project that goes beyond the stale rhetoric of the 'gift economy'. We can better describe it as an economy of attention and recognition. What really motivates Wikipedia collaborators, is the acknowledgement they receive from their peers, and the desire they have to see their skills recognized on a larger scale.[24]

Nonetheless, numerous elements of criticisms can be leveled against Wikipedia. Core contributors to the site start to behave like censors and wish to distinguish themselves from the mass of users (instead of helping them to build their own role in a creative fashion). Symptoms of hierarchy and domination appear within Wikipedia. There have been many conflicts among 'Wikipedians', and mass participation has given way to complex techno-bureaucracies which play a gatekeeping role. By now it is possible to dismiss the myth of Wikipedia as an online encyclope-

---

23  Geert Lovink, *The Principle of Notworking: Concepts in Critical Internet Culture,* Amsterdam: Amsterdam University Press, 2005, http://networkcultures.org/blog/publication/the-principle-of-notworking-geert-lovink/.

24  Felipe Ortega and Joaquin Rodriguez, *El Potlach digital, Wikipedia y el triumfo del procomun y el conocimiento compartido,* Madrid: Catedra, 2011.

dia that is the outcome of the collaboration of human beings all united by the same ideal. It is, even in absolute terms, mainly the collaboration between human beings and bots. Bots are small programs performing fully automated tasks without human intervention. Rambot, for instance, created over thirty thousand entries on cities in the world, extracting data from the CIA-published World Factbook and from US civil registries. As of now, bots account for 20% of the Wikipedia entries. [25] Wikipedia is better viewed as a highly complex socio-technical phenomenon, which is reminiscent of Bruno Latour's, notion of a 'parliament of things'. [26] Fans or detractors of Wikipedia, must both admit that social interaction in these systems is mediated through coded and automated processes, so that sensitive issues, such as the reliability of knowledge, are increasingly entrusted to machines. Then how does the hierarchy work between reliable and unreliable knowledge, human and 'bot' contributions? Source validation, protocols to resolve conflicts and common resource allocation are all pressing issues awaiting resolution.

Ultimately, despite the enormous differences, Wikipedia's modus operandi is still the same as that of the four giants of the digital world: Facebook, Amazon, Google and Apple. They all use the logic of accumulation, large numbers and the power of the masses. Even though they do not broadcast like traditional media they too aspire to hegemony. They compete fiercely because they want to win over a larger public and achieve a higher level of consensus. [27] When they praise the virtues of the 'long tail' made up of the millions of individuals who are dissatisfied with mass communication, they actually act as aggregators more interested in quantity than quality. Their ideal is the oxymoron of 'mass elitism'.

So, if it is essential to limit the number of participants for a space of conviviality to function properly, does that mean that the masses are condemned to triviality, self-promotion and self-exploitation as a consequence? The author of 'The Wisdom of Crowds', James Surowiecki, disagrees. In 'The Wisdom of Crowds', Surowiecki attempts to demonstrate that a randomly selected large group of people collectively possess superior skills to a small group of highly intelligent and well-prepared people. The concept of the wisdom of crowds does entail that a large group will

---

25  See: 'The Shadowy World of Wikipedia's Editing Bots', *MIT Technology Review*, February 2014, http://www.technologyreview.com/view/524751/the-shadowy-world-of-wikipedias-editing-bots/.

26  There is a wide range of issues, which are particularly difficult from a technical perspective, but central to the political and social debate, and are usually delegated to experts as they are considered too complex for ordinary people. The development of genetically modified organisms (GMOs), Internet governance, nuclear energy and the morning after pill are all products of techno-science and they play a substantial role in the construction of our reality. These products are created from scratch and create problems previously unthinkable (the ozone hole, the collaboration human-bots, fowl pest, one day the vaccine for AIDS...). Yet they still do not occupy a place in our imagination, since we have outsourced the technical management of these new phenomena. In this respect, Bruno Latour's work has been prophetic. See: Bruno Latour, *On the Modern Cult of the Factish Gods*, Durham: Duke University Press, 2009. Also see: Laura Bovone, 'Dai fatti ai fattici: conoscenza scientifica e senso commune oggi,' *Studi di Sociologia*, 2008, pp. 137-157.

27  The enthusiasm surrounding the war for technological supremacy is staggering. It is in a continuation of the most perverse aspect of capitalist competition, the idea that users benefit from fierce competition and should side for this or that charismatic leader. See the analysis of Farhad Manjoo, 'The Great Tech War Of 2012 – Apple, Facebook, Google, and Amazon Battle for the Future of the Innovation Economy, *Fast Company*, 19 October 2011, http://www.fastcompany.com/1784824/great-tech-war-2012.

always provide a better response, but that, on average, it will tend to produce a better solution than one individual alone could alone. In other words, a mixed crowd is, on average, apt to make better decisions than one expert. We have emphasized the need to question the role of experts, and even to turn their power back against the experts themselves. When technical knowledge is reserved or outsourced to specialized experts, they quickly lose the ability to realize their responsibility in the use of their knowledge-power. Each one of them relates exclusively to their own vested interests, their clients and their lobby's interests. At the same time access to knowledge is lost for the citizens and the common people.

There are several necessary conditions required for the collective wisdom of crowds to be expressed. Not all crowds are wise. Consider, for example, mobs or frenzied speculators in a stock market bubble. According to Surowiecki, these are the key criteria required to separate wise crowds from irrational ones: Diversity of opinion (Each person should have private information even if it's just an idiosyncratic interpretation of the known facts). Independence (People's opinions aren't determined by the opinions of those around them). Decentralization: (People are able to specialize and draw on local knowledge). Aggregation (Some mechanism exists for turning private judgments into a collective decision). [28]

Suriowecki emphasizes the importance of diversity ('as a value in itself'), and of independence, because the best collective decisions are the outcome of disagreement and discussions, not of pre-arranged consensus or compromises. By discussing very convincing examples, among them the development of the GNU/Linux operating system and the collaboration between laboratories worldwide leading to the discovery of SARS (Severe Acute Respiratory Syndrome), Surowiecki shows that, as paradoxical as it may seem to the conventional approach where the majority is lead by a minority representative, the intelligence of the group is superior provided that everyone in it acts in the most independent way possible. Individual autonomy is essential to a well functioning collective, provided that there is an agreement on the rules for sharing and the division of tasks.

But when one observes the concrete activities of an individual engaging with a social network, we see immediately that decision-making is not the only issue at stake. What is more important is to being on a common trajectory, spending time together, exploring the unknown in shared projects, meeting other people, and encountering the other. The crowd only becomes interesting when we get close up and discover the differences that make the many personal histories and form a collective narrative. Seen from afar, people are merely statistical figures or insignificant dots. [29] Participation is only worthwhile if individuals are part of a process of personal growth. On this issue there is no difference between the 'real' and the 'virtual' world. Surowiecki is useful to consider for the purposes our argument, in part because we do not share his exuberant faith in the masses, nor his concern for business.

Diversity is in fact more important in small groups and in informal organizations than in larger collectives, such as markets or electorates, simply because of the sheer size of most markets and

---

28   James Surowiecki, *The Wisdom of the Crowd*, Rome: Time Zones, p. 32.
29   See the discussion on the value of human life in Carlo Reed's *The Third Man* (1949). On top of the ferris wheel in the Prater in Vienna, Orson Welles tells Joseph Cotten, that from this vantage point human beings resemble dots that are interchangeable, and it would be insignificant if a few of them stopping moving forever.

the fact that anyone with money can enter them. This means that a minimum level of diversity is always ensured with a sufficiently large group. [30]

The issue of size is closely linked to the economy. There is a long tradition of thought shows that the project of economics, literally 'rule-norm-law of the house-environment' (and by extension, habitat) is irreconcilably at odds with 'ecology', which is the 'discourse on the house-environment-habitat'. In other words, a discourse that has the economy as its starting point cannot have social well-being as its aim, even if it pretends the contrary, because the social and the economic are grounded on different premises. Yet there has been no lack of attempts to appropriate the practices of social ecology in the economic sphere. Developing a new technology that has the potential to become highly profitable and widespread, is generally an effective way to gain access to energies and resources. [31]

In any case this belief is central to the 'Wikinomics' of Tapscott and Williams, and also the 'Social-nomics' of Qualman. [32] These new economic and social theories are based collaboration rather than competition. The main idea, touted as an epochal discovery, is that social collaboration generates more added value than competition. Outside the business world this observation would be deemed trivial at best but in the corporate sphere it was considered cutting edge. Wikinomics is based on four principles: openness, 'peering' (organizing 'independent' people within a company), sharing (firms must put their know-how at the disposal of their 'ecosystem' which is made up of clients, suppliers, and partners, in order to foster synergic growth), and acting globally (ignoring physical and geographical boundaries).

The most interesting concept in this is that of openness because it reveals the transformation of dynamic ecological equilibrium into economic exploitation. This is the logical outcome of the neo-liberal idea of freedom. In a similar manner the freedom of Free Software was quickly transformed into the profitable business of openness through the invention of Open Source. We discuss the difference between the two approaches in our first book, *Open non è Free*. [33] Like neoliberal companies, digital communities based around hacker ethics and global markets, realize their alleged freedom by opening up to the market. Hacker ethics, sharing and co-operation practices are used by the market, which has adopted hacker communities' developing methods in order to recover from the speculative trick of the net economy. The new words sound like the old ones, from 'free software' to 'open source', but the sense has completely changed: curiosity about new changes into permanent training; web fluidity into absolute flexibility; permanent connection for easy communication into a 24-hour work life. Everything is defined in terms of the global market's simple and effective slogans. The open society is being praised as an automatic product of the libertarian openness of online sociality. To be clear: we do not want to be open, we

30  James Surowiecki, *The Wisdom of the Crowd*, p. 51.

31  For an overview of the ambiguities in the technological framework of social ecology see: Murray Bookchin, *The Ecology of Freedom: The Emergence and Dissolution of Hierarchy*, Palo Alto: Cheshire Books, 1982. Especially chapters 9 and 10.

32  Don Tapscott and Anthony D Williams, *Wikinomics: How Mass Collaboration Changes Everything*, New York: Portfolio, 2006. An even more embarrassing analysis can be found in Erik Qualman, *Socialnomics: How Social Media Transforms the Way We Live and Do Business*, New York: Wiley, 2009.

33  Ippolita, *Open non è free*, Milan: Eleuthera, 2005.

would like to be free, or at least freer. For example, we do not want to be open to fascism, sexism, racism, authoritarianism of the left or right... in fact, openness has strictly nothing to do with a radical posture. Also philosophically speaking, as Karl Popper's works demonstrate, the Open Society is a liberal dream.

The boundaries of companies are now becoming increasingly porous and less secure. Outsourcing is commonplace, and the strict separation between work and leisure time is waning, not because technology takes time away from work in favor of socializing, but because every moment is now devoted to profit earning. Firms will hand out their employees mobile phones for free, unlimited call plans included, so that they are always reachable, always in touch with each other, and always productive even outside their paid working hours. They are in fact actors on permanent call, but not acknowledged as such. They are the true slaves of self-exploitation unleashed by the Wikinomics, automata who seamlessly write the immense serial novel of digital culture's while considering themselves as the stakeholders in the Internet's Collective Intelligence. They then feel compelled to adopt an absurd, totally Huxleyan posture, and to participate in the commonwealth by exercising their power as consumers. But if growth is mandatory, it might take little time before not going into debt will be considered immoral, and that calls for de-growth will be considered as a subversive activity.

If the masses are so intelligent and so eager to collaborate, then one could imagine that keyboard activism, dubbed as clicktivism and slacktivism, would be a residual phenomenon, and that mass democracy is just around the corner. But this is not the case, simply because a group does not necessarily function better than a single individual. The sum total of individuals with low skills, a lack of critical engagement, and little time to contribute to the building of a common world, will help generate a great number of clicks on banners ads, but give little hope to a rise in true collective participation.

Before the Silicon Valley hype about the wisdom of crowds, social psychologists had discovered that the performance of individuals in a group is often less efficient than working alone. Synergy is not a conditioned response. In 1882, the agricultural engineer Maximilien Ringelmann conducted the following experiment in the French countryside: four people were asked to pull on a rope, firstly all together, then one after the other. The rope was attached to a dynamometer (to measure the tensile force exerted). Ringelmann was surprised to discover that the sum of the individual tensile forces was significantly higher than that of the group. Several subsequent studies have confirmed this 'Ringelmann effect', and have shown that individuals of a group will generally become less productive as a group size increases. This non-synergic effect is most notable with simple, repetitive tasks, in which every link in the chain has an important role to play but easily is replaceable by anyone else. Applauding at a theater, voting, clicking on 'like', etc. follows the same dynamic. When individual differences are not highlighted and there is an increase in the number of participants, the results often become progressively worse. Why should we commit ourselves when anyone can click 'like' in our stead?

In a mass group we have no reason to distinguish ourselves since the identity of group is based on the norm, not by the exception. That is to say, an atomized individual, permanently taught to be interchangeable with any other 'atom', must develop standard characteristics to be attractive in the global market, in an endless repetition of the identical, with minor variations already included in the profiling system. Conversely, an autonomous individual will be more interesting because they are unique and possess specific characteristics, a particular mixture of different qualities and experiences. It is logical to think that such an individual will join various groups, not for the sake of self-promotion, but for the pleasure of sharing and meeting with other, like-minded individuals. To belong to a community, to an organized network functioning like a 'we' means to feel represented, not because you have the right to veto or vote, but because you have a direct influence on the network, because you can influence others and in turn be influenced by them. We swap experiences and make changes by building a common history together. This is a necessarily complex and dynamic equilibrium where mutual limits and boundaries are constantly renegotiated.

It is not possible to imagine individuals that are static and completely determined by the absolute principles of the libertarian market, acting perfectly and totally pre-programmed, fully complying to a group manifesto or mission statement. On the other hand, even an individual's extraordinary skills must find ways to harmonize in an organized network, because the mere size of the group does not necessarily result in decreased control. On the contrary, control at the minute level also exists in small group, and perhaps it is here where it reaches its peak intensity. A single person's error can determine the fate of the entire group. The discontent of one member can infect all others; conflicts then can grow out of proportions and overshadow any positive vision.

There is however, a big difference between control managed by automated systems with profit as motive, as in the case of mass profiling, and the mutual control exercised by members of a small group. In an affinity group the ties that form the network are also relationships based on trust. You know that you can have confidence in the judgments of others and use the group as a sounding board. Social control can then also function as a guarantee for individual autonomy, especially in times of discouragement and apathy, when an individual is no longer lucid and starts acting in ways that are reckless or destructive. As keepers of a shared history, and therefore also our own history, the others are the ones who can remind us that we have not always been in a state of suffering and despair. In the past we made significant contributions and there is no reason why we will not continue to do so in the future. Attention and recognition of individual creativity is the currency that circulates in an organized network. It is the time that we spend weaving these bonds that makes the experience invaluable.

## 3.06 — BEYOND TECHNOPHOBIA: LET'S BUILD CONVIVIAL TECHNOLOGIES TOGETHER!

Worldwide tribal chatter, the 'global village' imagined by McLuhan has now been realized. Our world is now Balkanized, fragmented in individual circles managed by corporate mega-machines. Technical apparatuses are presented as empowering extensions of our human body because 'technology is now part of our body' and it is impossible to do without it or to break free. McLuhan's analysis should be taken as a warning when faced with such a threatening system of domination:

Once we have surrendered our senses and nervous systems to the private manipulation of those who would try to benefit from taking a lease on our eyes and ears and nerves, we don't really have any rights left. [34]

---

34   Marshall McLuhan, *Understanding Media: The Extensions of Man*, Cambridge: MIT Press edition, 1994, p. 68.

Even before the issue of civic rights, it is firstly an issue of losing our personal autonomy, in terms of skills lost or ones that now will never develop. Forty years after such lucid insight by the Canadian sociologist, when the costs of this ubiquitous incapacitation should be obvious, the technological drift has enveloped itself around us in its ever more stifling coils. We are all sentient terminals of a global network and this integration process doesn't look like as it could be stopped. Even when we recognize the enormous problems the adoption of these technologies causes, there are very few possibilities to opt out. The escape routes considered by various commentators are not very convincing.

But we should not be deceived by the pressing demands for viable alternatives, especially when the demand is for alternatives that work immediately and are suitable for all. We should examine personal users need and whether an individual's desire, real or imaginary, can be satisfied. It is obvious that no alternatives exist if the quest is to for entity as large and powerful as Google. Only another Google could work as fast and efficiently as Google, just as an alternative social media platform that functions in the same way as Facebook would merely be a Facebook clone. Instead what is required are many niche alternatives and many local and diverse solutions. Gigantism simply does not work, nor does the ideology of unlimited growth and radical transparency will not set us free.

McLuhan's most famous dictum 'the medium is the message' cannot be taken seriously enough. The same message disseminated through different media undergoes change. The fact is, that in the digital society, we are the medium, and therefore message. Having debated about digital technologies we lost track of the depth of the changes that have occurred in the meanwhile. We have to return to the body, and that if our memories are stocked on line, our bodies will tend to materialize in those same places. To adapt oneself to the virtual world means, literally, to be absorbed and relocated elsewhere, often in the so-called data Clouds. The intangible lightness of being digitally connected cannot be dissociated from the server-banks' heaviness – data centers strewn around the planet, preferably in its colder regions, as computers heat up and need chilling. [35] Data centers are gigantic sheds with interconnected hard disks stacked up to the ceiling. These fragile monuments of total memory consume phenomenal amounts of electricity (3% of the US' total consumption in 2011), taking an equally phenomenal toll on the environment. Cloud computing will do nothing to mitigate this problem, since the exponential growth in data will undermine any attempt to reduce waste. [36] Each time we log into our digital profile to check whether we exist, somewhere another computer lights up, connecting our request over thousands of miles of cable, all so that we can 'connect' to our digital body.

The rapid transformation of millions of users into sentient terminals, incapable of surviving in a world without the web was made possible by the extraordinary adaptability of the human body. Until the middle of the 20th century, physical strength was an important criterion in a person's

---

35   Iceland, due to its massive geothermal and hydro resources, has become a location of choice for big IT players to build their data treatment centers. See: http://www.itworld.com/article/2735848/data-center/what-s-behind-iceland-s-first-major-data-center-.html.

36   See the report by the independent analyst firm Verdantix, 2 June 2011: Carbon Strategy Benchmark: Internet Sector. http://www.verdantix.com/index.cfm/papers/Products.Details/product_id/238/carbon-strategy-benchmark-it-services-sector.

employability. The technological promise of a world free of physical burdens has been realized for the richest part of the planet, who have adapted to a life between screens and keyboards. Meanwhile, the rest of the world aspires to participate in the pleasures of choosing between thousands of types of commodities. The consumer cult demands that we constantly use commodities as a form of identity and expression. Even the space occupied on remote servers is a status symbol and mark of identity. Occupying a lot of digital space results in having to manage a 'body' that stretches beyond the limits of physicality. In the context of corporate social media this body is subjected to default power, that is it is subjected to mandatory, unrequested influence. A digital body does not belong to users and can only be managed according to the rules imposed upon from the outside. Furthermore, the digital body has been shaped by the demands of the technological world which privilege brain power over physical strength. Google Earth is our all-seeing eye, but we may only use it, for free, within the limits granted to us. Meanwhile, our eyesight deteriorates as we keep sitting in front of a screen.

Theories of the brain, just like the theories of the body, have undergone dramatic change in recent years. Until a few decades ago the general idea was that, once its growth phase was over, the brain had become a static as an organ. Now we know that, on the contrary, the brain is extremely plastic and retains its plasticity throughout our life. Even though neurons keep dying, they continue to create new connections between existing neurons. The sensations we feel through repeated experience form new neuronal circuits, while neglected circuits eventually deteriorate. Even the thought of performing an action, to experience or re-experience a specific situation causes physical change on the neuronal level. Once these neuronal pathways are established it is nearly impossible to reverse such a change. In the case of social media, predominantly the eye and visual cortex is used, while the rest of the body becomes weaker. The brain adjusts accordingly, and so does our perception of the world. [37]

The brain is a muscle that when fed with too many superficial connections atrophies and loses other disused capacities. Just as junk food is a drug that upsets the metabolism, 'junk communication' pollutes the brain and overtime it is difficult to recover lost capabilities. [38] The concentration necessary to deep thinking requires quiet and attentiveness. Research has also demonstrated that cognitive capacities increase when in a natural environment. [39] More complex imaginative faculties, like empathy and compassion, need time and attention to develop and hone. The sight of another person's physical pain stimulates a response of empathy much more quickly than perceiving psychological pain, which is a more complex phenomena to grasp. [40] In terms of creativity, developing a common moral and aesthetic vision demands considerable time and an

37   Alvaro Pascual-Leone, Amir Amedi, Felipe Fregni and Lofti Merabet, 'The Plastic Human Brain Cortex', *Annual Review of Neurosciences*, 28 (2005): 377-401, http://brain.huji.ac.il/publications/Pascual-Leone_Amedi_et%20al%20Ann%20Rev%20Neurosci%2005.pdf.

38   See the overview in Nicolas Carr, *The Shallows: What the Internet is Doing to Our Brains*, New York: WW Norton & Company, 2010.

39   Marc G. Berman, John Jonides and Stephen Kaplan, 'The Cognitive Benefits of Interacting With Nature', *Psychological Science*, December 2008: 1207-1212, http://www.ncbi.nlm.nih.gov/pubmed/19121124.

40   Mary Helen Immordino-Yang, Andrea McColl, Hanna Damasio and Antonio Damasio, 'Neural Correlates of Admiration and Compassion', *Proceedings of the National Academy of Sciences*, 106:19 (2009): 8021-8026.

enormous listening capacity. It is easy to be angered and outraged by the injustices of the world, but it is near impossible to share dreams and utopias with technological tools that only generate distracted attention...

Our social dimension is not necessarily defined by current technologies. Mobile phones have become indispensable and the same is slowly happening with mass social media. But this is not necessarily inevitable. We could decide that we do not want to become dependent on Facebook or Google+ or any other social media platforms managed 'for our own good'. Instead we could try to find out together something better to nurture our social life, just as some people improve their diet. Our communication life could then become a deeply satisfying banquet instead of a void that becomes increasingly more difficult to fill.

A convivial information regimen is possible which favors the realization of individual freedom and empowerment within a society adequately equipped with efficient tools. The logical out-come of this critique of domination-oriented information is inevitably 'small is beautiful'; be-cause size matters. Beyond certain numbers, a fixed hierarchy becomes a requirement to man-age the relationships between human beings and other living beings in general. This is because everything that is in a relationship is 'relative'. If, instead of maintaining relationships with ten people, in a circumscribed space, we have to do with thousands or millions of people, relativity gives way to homology. To have one thousand friends does not make any sense at all since we do not have the time and energy to maintain all these so-called 'friendships'. Significant rela-tionships require time, attention and competence and cannot be satisfied, with the distracted attention or indifference characteristic of social media. Human beings can only effectively keep in touch, meaning here to know where are, what they do there etc., with a few dozen people at the same time.[41] In a project that has too high number of participants, people start to iden-tify categories of gender, 'race', wealth, resources, age, expertise, etc., in a fixed hierarchical manner. The standard white male discourse leaves no room for evolution other than through a radical break resulting in shocks, violence and disruptions which inevitably returns us to the question, what to do? This notorious Leninist question, 'What is to be done?' lacks any libertar-ian response without beginning yet another totalitarian revolution, from either the left or the right of the political spectrum.

Megamachines involves chain of both capitalist and despotic type. They create dependency, ex-ploitation, and powerlessness, reducing humans to the function of enslaved consumers. This is not a question of property issues, since:

> The collective ownership of the means of production does not alter anything in this state of affairs, and merely sustains a Stalinist despotic organization. Accordingly, Illich puts forward the alternative of everyone's right to make use of the means of production, in a 'convivial soci-ety', which is to say, a desiring and non-Oedipal society. This would mean the most extensive utilization of machines by the greatest number of people, the proliferation of small machines and the adaptation of the large machines to small units, the exclusive sale of machinic com-

---

41  Robin Dunbar, 'Coevolution of Neocortical Groupsize and Languages in Humans', *Behavioral and Brain Sciences*, 16 (1993): 681-735, http://www.uvm.edu/~pdodds/files/papers/others/1993/dunbar1993a.pdf.

ponents which would have to be assembled by the users-producers themselves, and the destruction of the specialization of knowledge and of the professional monopoly. [42]

The real question to ask then is how to do this? What are our desires in relation to digital technology? What kind of digital social networks, appropriate to our desires, would we like to build? Which tools will we use? Which modes of participation and of exchange would we like to draw upon?

We need to reverse the logic of radical transparency and apply it to the technologies we use, and to those social media platforms that promise immediate interaction but are in fact non-transparent intermediaries. It is absolutely essential for an individual to retain a private sphere and to nurture a secret, personal inner world that is not subject to profiling. It is vital to learn to spend time alone, in silence, and to learn to like each other, by facing the fear of the void, which social media tries to fill in vain. Only individuals that possess self-esteem and are happy with themselves, despite their flaws, will have the energy to build up sensible spaces of communication where they can meet other people. Only individuals who have acquired a know-how that goes beyond mere self-promotion skills, have something interesting to communicate and to share. Effective communication demands each person can listen to themselves, before even being able to listen to others. Algorithmic logic is both inadequate and degrading. It is not up to the individual to be transparent to technology; rather it is technological mediation itself that should be made to be as transparent and intelligible as possible. The process of constructing shared worlds must be explained.

Expressing desire is not an automatic process. Nor is the transmission of skills a spontaneous process. To formulate desires is not without risks. Relationships are based on trust and on the risk that this trust might be broken or betrayed. Stratification and depth are essential elements in a relationship. All forms of authentic communication are complex acts of sharing personal imagination. Misunderstandings are possible, and so-called radical transparency will not prevent conflicts from arising. It does not make sense to split up these processes into logical cycles and to submit them to the perfect algorithm. The automatic satisfaction of desires merely means outsourcing everything to technology, including the imagination. Welcome then to the desert of the automatic, induced desires, where there is nothing left to imagine.

There is a need to give an account of the communicative processes and of the technologies that implement them. We need to explore them with the help of texts and practices enabling us to extend, re-trace, and re-assemble the social, by making visible the mesh of connections between the social actors who are its protagonists. [43] This way it should be possible to cut across the now blocked instituted imaginary, and get it moving again. The net is the trace left by the flow of social assets and made visible by the constant translations performed by actors. Following these actors is certainly slower and more difficult for all-encompassing globalizing answers and main-streamed, standardizing theories, but it is a risk that must be taken in order to capture the

---

42   Gilles Deleuze and Felix Guattari, 'Balance Sheet-Program for Desiring Machines', *Semiotexte*, 2:3 (1977): 117-135.

43   This what we have tried to achieve in this text, using a methodology that in roughly following the sociological approach of Actor-Network theory. See Bruno Latour, *Reassembling the Social: an Introduction to Actor-Network-Theory*, Oxford: Oxford University Press, 2005.

complexity of the real. This book's ambition was to start sketching out the map of an area only partly explored, by following the connections between actors and their respective translations and betrayals. Naturally, the map does not always correspond with the territory, there are many empty spaces left, which may give rise to new associations. [44]

An actor carries out actions that are intended to achieve something. In this sense an actor is much more than a simple intermediary, since she is neither a neutral support nor an anonymous channel for external communication that does not result in any reaction or change. Quite on the contrary, an actor is a mediator who translates and modifies information, according to her own characteristics, and therefore is able to transmit messages in an effective way. Thus, when two friends have a banal conversation on Facebook chat, this not only involves the linguistic skills of two people, but also the ideology that underpins Facebook. The communication protocols of Facebook are layered in extremely complex networks and the mutual expectations of those who interact on the network, and many other aspects of interaction, are not all reducible to the catchall term 'information'.

It may appear strange to associate neurons, individuals, emotions, membranes and circuits, the macroscopic social world with the microscopic one of molecules, but in reality all these elements are connected. If anything it would be more unusual to dissociate them, strictly limiting individuals to the domain of sociology and anthropology, neurons to brain science, emotions to psychology, membranes to biology, and circuits to engineering or computer sciences. At this point it becomes impossible to identify the links between all these different elements, without resorting to an omnipresent essence, a deus ex machina of the social bond in the paradigm of informationalism. In other words, without speaking of imaginary 'social forces', or unidentified psychic forces, or history's 'manifest destiny' etc. Communication, however, does not transmit information, but requires the creation of spaces of interaction, in which heterogeneous actors are summoned together.

Collaboration can progressively evolve into convivial technology when it stops being part of the ongoing chatter and aims to create a shared space. Personal space can be developed both in an individual and in a collective sense. [45] If a space succeeds in giving individuals a sense of fulfillment, then it might be visited, shared, and used. Such a territory is a collective one; it represents a different system with regard to individuals. It is something that has not existed before, a radical

---

44   Rosi Braidotti, *Nomadic Subjects: Embodiment and Sexual Difference in Contemporary Feminist Theory*, 2nd Edition, New York: Columbia University Press, 2011.

45   Writing is a form of communication which build spaces of asynchronous interaction. Unlike speech, it does not require the simultaneous presence of the people being in communication. On the other hand, writing requires the use of various technological implements: a pen, a printing press, a computer, etc. Computer-mediated forms of collaborative writing, wikis for instance, or chat, mailing lists, etc., is a writing practice that can provide investigative methods to describe parts of reality in the making. In addition to this writing is also able to bring spaces into being where certain issues can acquire the degree of legitimacy needed in order to be asked. Convivial social spaces specifically built with this goal in mind, are places where individuals can meet each other, argue, possibly understand and influence each other, create together – and evolve in the process. See: Carlo Milani, *Scritture conviviali, Tecnologie per participare*, 2008, http://www.ippolita.net/sites/default/files/Scritture_conviviali-Carlo_Milani-2008. pdf.

creation, in the words of Castoriadis an imaginary institution, directed by a magmatic logic. [46] Using a convivial technology together means to change, to alter reality, to modify one's own reality, and in a broader sense, to change the world around us.

In the study of group dynamics, the largest problem, which may also sometimes be a strength, is the limits of the collective. [47] In all collaborative activities, the limits can be formulated in qualitative, quantitative, and temporal terms. Certain qualitative limits are self-evident, since collective work does conform to a specific individual's expectations but rather to the individual self as unfolding development within a collective self. It is, in a certain sense, less precise, as the perceptions of a single individual subject are not the same as those of the collective subject. Both subjects are in a process of coming-into-being and require a continuous and controlled exchange. For this reason doing things alone is much easier and less troublesome than doing them as a group. To operate within a group is painful in so far as you have to renounce having the final word, your own identity is under continuous re-assessment. The individual has to entrust a portion of their own self-expression to others. If one individual attempts to control everything, he stifle the collective and takes up a dominant role, he will be a constant point of criticism, even in those case where people end up agreeing with him.

It is essential to be exacting but there is a risk of becoming a 'guru', and even a censorious critic. Therefore it is essential to keep the group method in mind as a positive limit, which will also function as a quantitative limit with respect to the time and the energy that can be used sensibly in a collective activity. It will be even more difficult to achieve harmony in a project when there are large differences in the levels of personal investment in a project. Those who put in the most effort into a project are subsequently unable to do more and to compensate for the others' presumed or real failings. There are two reasons, related yet opposed, for this state of affairs. The first reason is external, the more you invest in a project the greater the risk that you will overshadow over participants and thwart autonomy within the collective. The second reason is internal; when an individual member takes on a disproportionate amount of responsibility, it becomes a source of frustration and they often demand compensation. 'I am doing all the work here' and 'nothing would happen without me' are the typical complaints of such an individual. But the others are unwilling to recognize these complaints, in order to not debase their own personal contribution or the collective. Seen from an economic perspective, doing more is not necessarily always a good a thing, cooperation demands the continuous renegotiation of the limits and the rules governing a collective.

Pure voluntarism is blind and often counter-productive. A sensible and constructive imbalance that tends towards chaos and the unexpected often requires us to step back in order to redistribute our energies in favor of others. This is not a matter of altruism, but simple tactic. Excessive imbalances should be avoided but on the other hand, we must also avoid adapting to the rhythm of participants who show the least enthusiasm and effort. Tempering enthusiasm often amounts to imposing a conservative viewpoint, in the sense of one that is already well established and not

---

46  See Cornelius Castoriadis, *The Imaginary Institution of Society*, trans. Kathleen Blamey, Cambridge, Mass: MIT Press, 1998.

47  See Marianella Sclavi, *Arte di ascoltare e mondi possibili: come si esce dalle cornici di cui siamo parte*, Pescara: Le vespe, 2000.

useful in overcoming difficulties. Enthusiasm should be encouraged with trust and trust must be balanced by a critical mindset, or in other words, by reflexivity. Mutual efforts should be directed towards developing a space of autonomy, and be fueled by pleasure rather a sense of duty or obligation. Otherwise frustration and resentment will gain the upper hand. The desire to dominate others is fed by the desire of others to be dominated, and vice-versa. This is why the balance needs to be dynamic and capable of drawing upon the energies of individual members, avoiding the crystallization of hegemonies and hierarchies. Stasis can only be overcome by appealing to the 'residual chaos', the imbalance regulated by shared procedures.

The compulsive tendency to return to the group must be restrained in a positive way. A group sometime needs to wind down, either to reconfigure itself or simply because it has spent all of its energy. Refined theories, flawless experiments, conducted by a collective without critical sense, are as beautiful as they are useless. Theories devoid of any critical relevance are merely ornamental and certainly not valuable tools. Perfectionism must be shunned when making room for the autonomy of what is to come. Instead we must embrace a contingent realism, defined by what technologies are currently available. The word games must stop when the mood has changed and the pleasure of playing and sharing have disappeared.

Facebook and similar social networks push us into disembodied mass elitism, which is synonymous with global totalitarianism organized in small, autarchic groups. Even though it is a complex laborious task, we prefer to take a risk and dare to imagine a world of convivial technologies. Everything is still possible; nothing is set in stone. We are here, with our desires and our time available to satisfy them. It is the right time to create something different. The moment has come to log out of social media, to go out on the streets and to start building different social networks.

# BIBLIOGRAPHY

Ackerman, Bruce and Yochai Benkler. 'Private Manning's Humiliation', *The New York Review of Books*, 28 April 2011, http://www.nybooks.com/articles/archives/2011/apr/28/private-mannings-humiliation/.

Allen, Jr., John L. 'Pope Cites Teilhardian Vision of the Cosmos as a 'Living Host', *National Catholic Reporter*, 28 July 2009, http://ncronline.org/news/pope-cites-teilhardian-vision-cosmos-living-host.

Anonymous. 'The Underground Myth', *Phrack Magazine*, 18 April 2008, http://phrack.org/issues/65/13.html.

Assange, Julian. *The Unauthorised Autobiography*, Edinburgh: Cannongate Books, 2011.

Bakunin, Mikhail. 'Man, Society, and Freedom', *Bakunin on Anarchy*, trans. Sam Dolgoff, London: Vintage Books, 1971.

Ballard, J.G. 'Which Way to Inner Space?', *New World Science Fiction*, vol. 40, Concrete Island, New York: Farrar, Straus and Giroux, 1998, pp 116-118.

Barabási, Albert-László. *Linked: The New Science of Networks*, New York: Perseus Book Groups, 2002.

Benderson, Bruce. *Transhumain*, Paris: Payot & Rivages, 2011.

Berman, Marc G., John Jonides and Stephen Kaplan. 'The Cognitive Benefits of Interacting With Nature', *Psychological Science*, December 2008: 1207-1212, http://www.ncbi.nlm.nih.gov/pubmed/19121124.

Bollier, David. *The Promise and Peril of Big Data*, Washington: The Aspen Institute, 2011, http://www.aspen-institute.org/sites/default/files/content/docs/pubs/The_Promise_and_Peril_of_Big_Data.pdf.

Boni, Stefano. *Cuture e Poteri*, Milan: Eleuthera, 2011, p. 29-33.

Bookchin, Murray. *The Ecology of Freedom: The Emergence and Dissolution of Hierarchy*, Palo Alto: Cheshire Books, 1982.

Boshmaf, Yazan, Ildar Muslukhov, Konstantin Beznosov, and Matei Ripeanu. 'The Socialbot Network: When Bots Socialize for Fame and Money', *Proceedings of the 27th Annual Computer Security Applications Conference (ACSAC'11)*, December 2011, http://lersse-dl.ece.ubc.ca/record/264/files/ACSAC_2011.pdf.

Bovone, Laura. 'Dai fatti ai fattici: conoscenza scientifica e senso commune oggi,' *Studi di Sociologia*, 2008.

Boyd, Danah. *Facebook and Radical Transparency (a rant)*, 14 May 2010, http://www.zephoria.org/thoughts/archives/2010/05/14/Facebook-and-radical-transparency-a-rant.html.

Boyd Danah, and Kate Crawford. 'Six Provocations for Big Data', *A Decade in Internet Time: Symposium on the Dynamics of the Internet and Society*, September 2011, http://papers.ssrn.com/sol3/papers.cfm?abstract_id=1926431.

Boyd, Danah M. and Nicole B. Harison. 'Social Network Sites: Definition, History, and Scholarship', *Journal of Computer-Mediated Communications*, 13:1 (October 2007): 210-230.

Braidotti, Rosi. *Metamorphoses: Towards a Materialist Theory of Becoming*, Cambridge: Polity Press, 2002.

Braidotti, Rosi. *Nomadic Subjects: Embodiment and Sexual Difference in Contemporary Feminist Theory*, 2nd Edition, New York: Columbia University Press, 2011.

Campbell, Duncan. *Électronique Planétaire*, Paris: Editions Allia, 2001.

Carr, Nicolas. *The Shallows: What the Internet is Doing to Our Brains*, New York: WW Norton & Company, 2010.

Castells, Manuel. *The Rise of The Network Society: The Information Age: Economy, Society and Culture*, Hoboken: John Wiley & Sons, 2000.

Castoriadis, Cornelius. *La Societé bureaucratique*, Paris: Bourgois, 1990.

Castoriadis, Cornelius. *The Imaginary Institution of Society*, trans. Kathleen Blamey, Cambridge: MIT Press, 1997.

de Certeau, Michel. *The Practice of Everyday Life*, trans. Steven Rendall, Berkeley: University of California Press, 1984.

Coleman, Gabriella. 'Hacker Politics and Publics', *Public Culture*, New York: Institute of Public Knowledge, 2011, http://gabriellacoleman.org/wp-content/uploads/2012/08/Coleman-hacker-politics-publics.pdf.

Cook, John. 'Is Zynga's Culture Really Rotten at the Core? Hear how Mark Pincus Described the Mission in April', *Geekwire*, 28 November 2011, http://www.geekwire.com/2011/zyngas-culture-rotten-core/.

da Costa, Beatriz, 'Amateur Science: A Threat After All?', 2005, http://rixc.lv/reader/txt/txt.php?id=149&l=en.

Cyrulnik, Boris. *Ensorcellement du monde*, Paris: Odile Jacob, 1997.

Cyrulnik, Boris. *Les nourritures affective,* Paris: Odile Jacob, 2000.

Cyrulnik, Boris. *De chair et d'âme,* Paris: Odile Jacob, 2006.

Das, Anupreeta, Robert Frank and Liz Rappaport. 'Facebook Flop Riles Goldman Clients', *The Wallstreet Journal*, 19 January 2011, http://online.wsj.com/article/SB10001424052748703954004576090440048416766.html#articleTabs%3Darticle.

Davies, Nick. '10 Days in Sweden: the Full Allegations Against Julian Assange', *The Guardian*, 17 December 2010, http://www.theguardian.com/media/2010/dec/17/julian-assange-sweden.

Deleuze, Gilles and Felix Guattari. 'Balance Sheet-Program for Desiring Machines', *Semiotexte*, 2:3 (1977): 117-135.

Domscheit-Berg, Daniel. *Inside WikiLeaks: My Time with Julian Assange at the World's Most Dangerous Website*, New York: Crown, 2011.

Dunbar, Robin. 'Coevolution of Neocortical Groupsize and Languages in Humans', *Behavioral and Brain Sciences*, 16 (1993): 681-735, http://www.uvm.edu/~pdodds/files/papers/others/1993/dunbar1993a.pdf.

Eckersley, Peter. 'How Unique is Your Web browser?', *Proceeding PETS'10 Proceedings of the 10th International Conference on Privacy Enhancing Technologies*, Springer, 2010, https://panopticlick.eff.org/browser-uniqueness.pdf.

Feyerabend, Paul. *Against Method. Outline of an Anarchist Theory of Knowledge*, 4th ed., New York: Verso Books, 2010.

Foreman, Richard. 'The Pancake People, or, the God's Are Pounding on My Head', *Edge*, 3 August 2005, http://edge.org/3rd_culture/foreman05/foreman05_index.html.

Galbraith, John Kenneth. *The Anatomy of Power*, Boston: Houghton Mifflin, 1983.

Galison, Peter. 'Removing Knowledge', *Critical Inquiry*, 31 (2004) Chicago: University of Chicago Press, https://www.fas.harvard.edu/~hsdept/bios/docs/Removing%20Knowledge.pdf.

Galison, Peter. *Secrecy*, http://www.secrecyfilm.com/about.html.

Galloway, Alexander R. and Eugene Thacker. *The Exploit: A Theory of Networks*, Minneapolis: University of Minnesota Press, 2007.

Greenberg, Andy. 'An Interview With WikiLeaks' Julian Assange', *Forbes Magazine*, 29 November 2010, http://www.forbes.com/sites/andygreenberg/2010/11/29/an-interview-with-WikiLeaks-julian-assange/5.

Groeger, Lena. 'SpyCloud: Intel Agencies Look to Keep Secrets in the Ether', *Wired*, 29 Jun 2011, http://www.wired.com/2011/06/spycloud-intel-agencies-look-to-keep-secrets-in-the-ether/.

Grohol, John M. 'FOMO Addiction: The Fear of Missing Out', *Psych Central*, 2013, http://psychcentral.com/blog/archives/2011/04/14/fomo-addiction-the-fear-of-missing-out/.

Gruppo MARCUSE. *Miseria Humana Della Publicità*, Milan: Eleuthera, 2006.

Gubitosa, Carlo. *Italian Crackdown: BS amatoriali, volontari telematici, censure e sequestri nell'Italia degli anni '90*, Milan: Apogeo, 1999.

Harraway, Donna. 'A Cyborg Manifesto, Science, Technology, and Socialist-Feminism in the late Twentieth Century', *Simians, Cyborgs, and Women: the Reinvention of Nature*, New York: Routledge, 1991, http://www.egs.edu/faculty/donna-haraway/articles/donna-haraway-a-cyborg-manifesto.

Hodgkinson, Tom. 'With Friends Like These…', *The Guardian*, 14 January 2008, http://www.theguardian.com/technology/2008/jan/14/facebook.

Ibañez, Tomàs. *Il Libero Pensiero. Elogio del Relativismo*, Milan: Elèuthera, 2007.

Illich, Ivan. *Tools for Conviviality*, London: Fontana, 1975 (1973).

Immordino-Yang, Mary Helen, Andrea McColl, Hanna Damasio and Antonio Damasio. 'Neural Correlates of Admiration and Compassion', *Proceedings of the National Academy of Sciences*, 106:19 (2009): 8021-8026.

Ippolita. *Nell'acquario di Facebook*, Milan: Ledizioni, 2012.

Ippolita. *Open non è free,* Milan: Eleuthera, 2005.

Ippolita. *The Dark Side of Google,* trans. Patrice Riemens, Amsterdam: Institute of Network Cultures, Theory on Demand #13, 2013, http://networkcultures.org/blog/publication/no-13-the-dark-side-of-google-ippolita/.

Ippolita, Geert Lovink and Ned Rossiter. 'The Digital Given. 10 Theses on Web 2.0', *The Fiberculture Journal 14* (2009), http://fourteen.fibreculturejournal.org/fcj-096-the-digital-given-10-web-2-0-theses/.

Irigaray, Luce. *Sharing the World,* London: Continuum, 2008.

Jennings, Richi. 'Anonymous Antisec hacks STRATFOR in Lulzxmas operation', *Computerworld,* 27 December 2011, http://www.computerworld.com/article/2471899/cybercrime-hacking/anonymous-antisec-hacks-stratfor-in-lulzxmas-operation.html.

Khouri, Rami G. 'When Arabs Tweets', *International Herald Tribune,* 22 July 2010, http://www.nytimes.com/2010/07/23/opinion/23iht-edkhouri.html.

Kirkpatrick, David. *The Facebook Effect,* New York: Simon & Schuster, 2009.

Klein, Naomi. 'China's All-Seeing Eye', *Rolling Stone Magazine,* 14 May 2008, http://www.naomiklein.org/articles/2008/05/chinas-all-seeing-eye.

La Cecla, Franco. *Sorrogati di presenza. Media e vita quotidiana,* Milan: Mondadori, 2006.

Lacy, Sarah. 'Peter Thiel: We're in a Bubble and It's Not the Internet. It's Higher Education', *Techcrunch,* 10 April 2010, http://techcrunch.com/2011/04/10/peter-thiel-were-in-a-bubble-and-its-not-the-internet-its-higher-education/.

Lanier, Jaron. 'The Hazards of Nerd Supremacy: The Case of WikiLeaks', *The Atlantic,* 20 December 2010, http://www.theatlantic.com/technology/archive/2010/12/the-hazards-of-nerd-supremacy-the-case-of-WikiLeaks/68217/.

Laplantine, François. *Je, Nous et les autres. Etres humains au-delà des appartenances,* Paris: Le Pommier, 1999 Laplantine, François. *Le Sujet: essai d'anthropologie politique,* Paris: Éditions Téraèdre, 2007.

Latour, Bruno. *On the Modern Cult of the Factish Gods,* Durham: Duke University Press, 2009.

Latour, Bruno. *Reassembling the Social: an Introduction to Actor-Network-Theory,* Oxford: Oxford University Press, 2005.

Lattman, Peter. 'Why Facebook Is Such a Crucial Friend for Goldman', *New York Times,* 3 January 2011, http://dealbook.nytimes.com/2011/01/03/why-Facebook-is-such-an-important-friend-for-goldman-sachs/.

Lévy, Pierre. *Collective Intelligence,* New York: Basic Books, 1995.

Levy, Steven. *Hackers, Heroes of the Computer Revolution,* New York: Penguin, 1984.

Lovink, Geert. *The Principle of Notworking: Concepts in Critical Internet Culture,* Amsterdam: Amsterdam University Press, 2005, http://networkcultures.org/blog/publication/the-principle-of-notworking-geert-lovink/.

Lovink, Geert and Patrice Riemens. 'Twelve Theses on WikiLeaks,' *Eurozine Magazine,* July 2010, http://www.eurozine.com/articles/2010-12-07-lovinkriemens-en.html.

Luttwak, Edward. *Turbo-Capitalism: Winners and Losers in the Global Economy,* New York: Harpers, 1999.

Manjoo, Farhad. 'The Great Tech War Of 2012 – Apple, Facebook, Google, and Amazon Battle for the Future of the Innovation Economy, *Fast Company,* 19 October 2011, http://www.fastcompany.com/1784824/great-tech-war-2012.

Martin, Brian. 'Grassroots Science', Sal Restivo (ed.), *Science, Technology, and Society: An Encyclopedia,* Oxford: Oxford University Press, 2005, http://www.bmartin.cc/pubs/05Restivo.html.

Maurizi, Marco. 'Che cos' è l'antispecismo', *Liberazioni,* no 4, February 2008, http://www.liberazioni.org/articoli/MauriziM-06.htm.

Mayer-Schönberger, Viktor. *The Virtue of Forgetting in the Digital Age,* New Jersey: Princeton University Press, 2009.

McKeon, Matt. 'The Evolution of Privacy on Facebook', http://mattmckeon.com/facebook-privacy/.

McLuhan, Marshall. *Understanding Media: The Extensions of Man,* Cambridge: MIT Press edition, 1994.

McPherson, Miller, Lynn Smith-Lovin and James M. Cook. 'Birds of a Feather: Homophily in Social Networks', *Annual Review of Sociology,* vol 27: 415-444, August 2001, http://www.annualreviews.org/doi/abs/10.1146/annurev.soc.27.1.415.

Menn, Joseph, Francesco Guerrera and Shannon Bond. 'Goldman Deal Values Facebook at $50bn', *Financial Times,* 4 January 2011, http://www.ft.com/cms/s/0/e0dad322-173c-11e0-badd-00144feabdc0.html#axzz1KzW89fTA.

Milani, Carlo. *Scritture conviviali, Tecnologie per participare*, 2008, http://www.ippolita.net/sites/default/files/Scritture_conviviali-Carlo_Milani-2008.pdf.

Monbiot, George, 'This Bastardised Libertarianism Makes 'Freedom' an Instrument of Oppression', *The Guardian*, 19 December 2011.

Mumford, Lewis. *The Pentagon of Power: The Myth of the Machine, Vol. II.*, New York: Harcourt Brace Jovanovich, 1970.

Naone, Erica. 'The Changing Nature of Privacy on Facebook' *MIT Technology Review*, May 2010, http://www.technologyreview.com/news/418766/the-changing-nature-of-privacy-on-facebook/.

Narayanam, Arvind and Vitaly Shmatikov. 'De-anonymizing Social Networks,' *Proceedings of the 2009 30th IEEE Symposium on Security and Privacy*, pp. 173-187, http://www.computer.org/csdl/proceedings/sp/2009/3633/00/3633a173-abs.html.

O'Brien, Jeffrey M. 'The PayPal Mafia', *Fortune*, 13 November 2007, http://fortune.com/2007/11/13/PayPal-mafia/.

Oliver, J. Michael and Stone Donald C,'Exclusive Interview with Murray Rothbard', originally published in *The New Banner: A Fortnightly Libertarian Journal*, 25 February 1972, http://archive.lewrockwell.com/rothbard/rothbard103.html.

Orlowski, Andrew. 'Cryptome: PayPal a "Liar, Cheat and a Thug"', *The Register*, 10 March 2010, http://www.theregister.co.uk/2010/03/10/cryptome_PayPal/.

Ortega, Felipe and Joaquin Rodriguez. *El Potlach digital, Wikipedia y el triumfo del procomun y el conocimiento compartido*, Madrid: Catedra, 2011.

Pascual-Leone, Alvaro, Amir Amedi, Felipe Fregni and Lofti Merabet. 'The Plastic Human Brain Cortex', *Annual Review of Neurosciences*, 28 (2005): 377-401, http://brain.huji.ac.il/publications/Pascual-Leone_Amedi_et%20al%20Ann%20Rev%20Neurosci%2005.pdf.

Pedreschi, Dino et al. 'Big Data Mining, Fairness and Privacy: A Vision Statement Towards an Interdisciplinary Roadmap of Research', *KD Nuggets*, October 2011, http://www.kdnuggets.com/2011/10/big-data-mining-fairness-privacy.html.

Qualman, Erik. *Socialnomics: How Social Media Transforms the Way We Live and Do Business*, New York: Wiley, 2009.

Raymond, Eric S. *The Jargon File*, https://web.archive.org/web/20130827121341/http://cosman246.com/jargon.html.

Rediker, Marcus. *Villains of All Nations: Atlantic Pirates in the Golden Age*, London: Verso, 2004.

Raymond, Eric S. 'Homesteading the Noosphere', *The Cathedral & the Bazaar*, California: O'Reilly, 1999, http://www.catb.org/esr/writings/homesteading/homesteading.

Riemens, Patrice. 'Some Thoughts on the Idea of "Hacker Culture"', http://cryptome.org/hacker-idea.htm; original article: 'Quelques réflexions sur la "culture hacker"', *Multitudes* 1:8 (2002): 181-187.

Rothbard, Murray N. 'Praxeology: The Methodology of Austrian Economics', *The Logic of Action One Method, Money, and the Austrian School*, Cheltenham: Elgar, 1997, https://mises.org/rothbard/praxeology.pdf. See, https://www.facebook.com/help/search/?query=real%20names.

Sclavi, Marianella. *Arte di ascoltare e mondi possibili: come si esce dalle cornici di cui siamo parte*, Pescara: Le vespe, 2000.

Sloterdijk, Peter. 'Rules for the Human Zoo. A Response to the Letter on Humanism', *Environment and Planning D: Society and Space*, 27 (2009): 12-28, http://rekveld.home.xs4all.nl/tech/Sloterdijk_RulesForTheHumanZoo.pdf.

Sterling, Bruce. *The Hacker Crackdown: Law and Disorder on the Electronic Frontier*, New York: Bantam Books, 1992, http://www.mit.edu/hacker/hacker.html.

Surowiecki, James. *The Wisdom of the Crowd*, Rome: Time Zones, 2007.

Tan, Leon. 'The Pirate Bay: Countervailing Power and the Problem of State Organized Crime', *C Theory*, November 2010, http://www.ctheory.net/articles.aspx?id=672.

Tapscott, Don and Anthony D. Williams, *Wikinomics: How Mass Collaboration Changes Everything*, New York: Portfolio, 2006.

Thiel, Peter. 'The Education of a Libertarian', *Cato Unbound*, 13 April 2009, http://www.cato-unbound.org/2009/04/13/peter-thiel/education-libertarian.

Thiel, Peter. 'End of the Future', *National Review*, 3 October 2011, http://www.nationalreview.com/article/278758/end-future-peter-thiel.

Thiel, Peter. 'The Optimistic Thought Experiment', *Policy Review*, 29 January 2008, http://www.hoover.org/research/optimistic-thought-experiment.

Tilly, Charles and Sidney Tarrow. *Contentious Politics*, Boulder: Paradigm Publishers, 2007.

Wesoff, Eric. 'Peter Thiel Doesn't Like Cleantech VC, Mankind', *Green Tech Media*, 14 September 2011, http://www.greentechmedia.com/articles/read/peter-thiel-doesnt-like-cleantech-mankind.

Zittrain, Jonathan, Lawrence Lessig, et al. 'Radio Berkman 171: WikiLeaks and the Information Wars', *MediaBerkman*, 8 December 2010, http://blogs.law.harvard.edu/mediaberkman/2010/12/08/radio-berkman-171/.

*Works with an Anonymous or Unknown Author*

'Free Speech Case Study: The Demise of Tomaar.net', *Anonymous Proxies*, February 2011, http://www.anonymous-proxies.org/2011/02/free-speech-risks-demise-of-tomaarnet.html.

'The Goldman Sachs Facebook Deal: Is This Business as Usual?', *Public Policy*, 19 January 2011, http://knowledge.wharton.upenn.edu/article/the-goldman-sachs-facebook-deal-is-this-business-as-usual/.

H.R. 3261 (112th). 'Stop Online Piracy Act', October 2011, https://www.govtrack.us/congress/bills/112/hr3261/text.

'L'intervento di Moeed Ahmad', *Al Jazeera e i nuevi media*, 27 April 2010, http://www.dailymotion.com/video/xd3jl5_al-jazeera-e-i-nuovi-media-l-interv_news%20.

Pirate Party Declaration of Principles 3.2, http://docs.piratpartiet.se/Principles%203.2.pdf.

'The Shadowy World of Wikipedia's Editing Bots', *MIT Technology Review*, February 2014, http://www.technologyreview.com/view/524751/the-shadowy-world-of-wikipedias-editing-bots/.

'Swedish Pirate Party to Host New WikiLeaks Servers', *Piratpartiet Presscenter*, August 2010, http://press.piratpartiet.se/2010/08/17/swedish-pirate-party-to-host-new-WikiLeaks-servers/.

'The Threat from the Internet: Cyberwar', *The Economist*, July, 2010, http://www.economist.com/node/16481504.

# THANKS

We thank Monique Slodzian, Mathieu Valette and all the researchers at INALCO. Miguel and Virus Editorial for our tour in Spain, where this text got started, and all those who contributed from Barcelona, Pamplona, Madrid, Seville, Zaragoza, Bilbao, Santander, Oviedo, Xigon. Lidia. The Vogogna patio, La Scighera, Au Canut le 26, Alekos.net, Alberto, Carla, CEDRATS (Lyon), Mimmo & Christian, and the House of Baires for logistics support. LSH, Vivien, Pino, Maria, Saretta, Casanostra, Martarossa, Catecara, Spaziogiorgio, Patrice (+4D – now 5!), Spideralex, Fascema, Lorenzo, Korta. V.

++++++++++++++++++

You'll Never Walk Alone

Geert Lovink, Giovanna Cosenza, Vecna, Apuleius, Peter Sloterdijk, Donna Haraway, Boris Vian, Luciano di Samosata, danah boyd, James G. Ballard, Carl Off, Rosi Braidotti, Ivan Illich, William Gibson, Biella Coleman, CAE, Andrea Salsedo, Christa Wolf, Moebius, Paul K. Feyerabend, Marion Z. Bradly, Manuel Castells, Robert Nesta, Gilles Deleuze, Ursula Le Guin, Italo Calvino, Cornelius Castoriadis, Assata Shakur, Friedrich Dürrenmatt, François Laplantine, Maja Gimbutas, Michel de Certeau, Freddie Mercury, Moacyr Scliar, Elias Canetti, Maurice Ravel, Aphex Twin, Roberto Bolaño, Ilya Prigogine, Hannah Arendt, Tomàs Ibañez, Michael Ende, Humberto R. Maturana, Darth Vader.

Please address all your queries, comments and complaints to info@ippolita.net.

Translated (Q&D) by Patrice Riemens. This translation project is supported and facilitated by the Institute of Network Cultures, Amsterdam University of Applied Sciences (http://networkcultures. org/), the Antenna Foundation, Nijmegen (http://www.antenna.nl) and Casa Nostra, Vogogna-Ossola, Italy.